RESEARCH-BASED STRATEGIES TO

IGNTE

STUDENT LEARNING

INSIGHTS FROM A NEUROLOGIST AND CLASSROOM TEACHER

JUDY WILLIS, M.D.

D0973442

ASCD

Alexandria, Virginia USA

1703 N. Beauregard St. • Alexandria, VA 22311-1714 USA
Phone: 800-933-2723 or 703-578-9600 • Fax: 703-575-5400
Web site: www.ascd.org • E-mail: member@ascd.org
Author guidelines: www.ascd.org/write

Gene R. Carter, *Executive Director;* Nancy Modrak, *Director of Publishing;* Julie Houtz, *Director of Book Editing & Production;* Deborah Siegel, *Project Manager;* Reece Quiñones, *Senior Graphic Designer;* Keith Demmons, *Desktop Publishing Specialist;* Dina Seamon, *Production Specialist/Team Lead*

All Web links in this book are correct as of the publication date below but may have become inactive or otherwise modified since that time. If you notice a deactivated or changed link, please e-mail books@ascd.org with the words "Link Update" in the subject line. In your message, please specify the Web link, the book title, and the page number on which the link appears.

ASCD Member Book, No. FY06-09 (August 2006, P). ASCD Member Books mail to Premium (P), Comprehensive (C), and Regular (R) members on this schedule: Jan., PC; Feb., P; Apr., PCR; May, P; July, PC; Aug., P; Sept., PCR; Nov., PC; Dec., P.

PAPERBACK ISBN-13: 978-1-4166-0370-2   ASCD product #107006
PAPERBACK ISBN-10: 1-4166-0370-0
Also available as an e-book through ebrary, netLibrary, and many online booksellers (see Books in Print for the ISBNs).

Quantity discounts for the paperback edition only: 10–49 copies, 10%; 50+ copies, 15%; for 1,000 or more copies, call 800-933-2723, ext. 5634, or 703-575-5634. For desk copies: member@ascd.org.

Library of Congress Cataloging-in-Publication Data

Willis, Judy.
  Research-based strategies to ignite student learning : insights from a neurologist and classroom teacher / Judy Willis.
      p. cm.
  Includes bibliographical references.
  ISBN-13: 978-1-4166-0370-2 (pbk. : alk. paper)
  ISBN-10: 1-4166-0370-0 (pbk. : alk. paper) 1. Learning, Psychology of. 2. Learning–Physiological aspects. 3. Brain. I. Title.

  LB1060.W545 2006
  370.15'23–dc22

                                        2006013341

15 14   6 7 8 9 10 11 12

---

*To Paul, my college sweetheart of
35 years, for encouraging my career change
and the writing of this book. I love your
humor and honor, wisdom, and good taste in
wine, women, and dogs.*

RESEARCH-BASED STRATEGIES TO

IGNITE

STUDENT LEARNING

INSIGHTS FROM A NEUROLOGIST AND CLASSROOM TEACHER

PREFACE

The events in our lives happen in a sequence in time but in their significance to ourselves they find their own order . . . the continuous thread of revelation.

~ Eudora Welty

Now is an exciting and pivotal time to be an educator. Neuroimaging and brain mapping research has extended beyond the confines of studying medical and psychological diseases and has opened windows into the brain. We can now see brain activity as information from the senses that is categorized and organized into working, relational, and, ultimately, long-term memories. In short, we can now see what happens to brain activity and structure when teachers teach and when students learn. Educators can now relate the powerful discoveries of learning brain research to classrooms and curriculum by incorporating research-based learning strategies to help students learn more effectively and joyfully. The potential for discovering the most effective ways to educate students is unlimited.

These chapters demonstrate specific classroom strategies that have been developed from research in how the brain accumulates, connects, stores, and retrieves learned material. Information obtained through brain imaging such as positron emission tomography (PET scans), functional magnetic resonance imaging (fMRI), and quantitative electroencephalography brain wave monitoring (qEEG) during the learning process have given us a *science* of education to add to our already powerful knowledge of the *art* of teaching. Educational professionals who understand the relevant aspects of brain development, alertness, attention, and memory storage and retrieval, and who use the strategies derived from this research, will find their work becoming more effective and exciting and will find their students more engaged.

My personal revelations about the brain started not as a classroom teacher but as a neuroscience researcher during my premedical years at Williams College. There, in 1970, I used one of the first generation of electron microscopes to look at synapses connecting brain cells in the cerebral cortex in the brains of chicks. I was looking for a visible change in brain structure associated with learning. My heart still races as I recall the night I sat alone in the darkroom of the science center developing my electron micrographs and saw a greater collection of protein in the synapses of chicks that had been imprinted (had learned) to follow a moving light. It was like seeing something that had been, until that moment, only an abstract concept.

In the ensuing 35 years, I attended UCLA Medical School and became a neurologist in clinical practice treating children and adults with a wide spectrum of dysfunctions in their nervous systems. My work was fascinating, and especially exciting were the innovations in neuroimaging that became available to practicing physicians during those years, from the early computerized tomography (CT) and magnetic resonance imaging (MRI) scans, to brain mapping through specialized electroencephalogram (EEG), to the more recent decades of PET scanning and functional MRI scans.[1]

As my daughters went through their early school years, I found myself drawn to the dynamic classrooms of gifted teachers. I went from being a physician and mom who volunteered a few hours a week to being an occasional substitute teacher, and finally went back to being a student myself. I attended the Gevirtz Graduate School of Education at the University of California, Santa Barbara, where I earned my teaching credential and master's degree in education. I had come full circle and was back to studying the process and products of learning, only this time it was in children, not chicks.

During my six years as a full-time classroom teacher in elementary and middle school, I have continued to practice neurology during school vacations. The focus of my academic reading is no longer predominantly on neurological diseases, but rather on the neuroscientific studies of the learning process. Unfortunately, as with many scientific discoveries, the information that brain-imaging tools have yielded has sometimes been misinterpreted and misrepresented by nonscientists.

Every day there are new claims of ways to improve learning and memory, from herbs and vitamins to meditation and hypnosis.

As I compared the claims of some self-proclaimed educational experts with the actual neurology research, I found many disconnects between the objective scientific data and the interpretations and conjectures made by people lacking the scientific background to properly assess the research. I became concerned about some of the conclusions being made and recommendations for strategies being proposed as "scientific." How are teaching professionals to know which of these are valid? How can teachers learn about and ultimately create their own strategies based upon reliable brain-based learning research?

I realized that my background in neuroscience and education could help other education professionals gain the neuroscientific background to evaluate for themselves the brain research and the associated claims. After writing about the neuroscience of learning for educational journals, and speaking at conferences and seminars, I followed the requests of my colleagues to compile the material into this book. I have included information about the exciting discoveries relating to the brain activity that occurs during all aspects of the learning process. The major focus of this book, however, is to help educators acquire or hone strategies to guide students' brains to more effective focusing; sustained attentiveness; and active learning, storing, connecting, and retrieval of learned material. In each chapter you'll find a few brief sections titled "Gray Matter." These sections give more in-depth, technical information for readers who are interested in exploring the neuroscience that underscores the teaching strategies provided.

As you learn more about brain-based teaching and learning strategies, you'll find yourself discovering greater joy and renewed enthusiasm in your classroom, school administration, and curriculum planning because you will have added a new or greater dimension to your skills as an educational professional. Starting with chapters about brain-based strategies for attention focusing and memory building, and moving through more specific applications of these techniques for students with learning differences, attention disorders, varied learning styles, and gifted and challenged students, you will find support for strategies you currently use and recognize the value of new ones.

Other chapters will consider your role as an informed educator with the potential to shape educational policy during one of the most pivotal times in the history of education. You are in the field of education at the exciting yet challenging time when science is discovering or confirming the most effective brain-based teaching strategies.

Simultaneously, partisan politicians are becoming more intrusive in legislating what outcomes are expected for our students. It will be the obligation of education professionals informed in the science and art of education to use their understanding of valid research, together with their professional skills and experience, to keep critical educational decisions in the domain of professional educators. Your own expertise and accurate understanding of brain-based learning strategies, from neuroimaging and brain mapping, will increase your expertise on what constitutes the best educational techniques for students. The greater your understanding and participation in the decisions being made now, the less power politicians looking for political capital will have to serve their own needs by manipulating our country's most valuable natural resource—our children.

Note

1. Through functional brain imaging we can see the neural activity in particular brain regions as the brain performs discrete cognitive tasks. These images enable scientists to match brain function with structure and location. The CT scan (computerized tomography scan) uses a narrow beam of X-rays to create brain images displayed as a series of brain slices. In a PET (positron emission tomography) scan, radioactive isotopes are injected into the blood attached to molecules of glucose. As a part of the brain is more active, its glucose and oxygen demands increase. The isotopes attached to the glucose give off measurable emissions used to produce maps of areas of brain activity. The higher the radioactivity count, the greater the activity taking place in that portion of the brain. Quantitative EEG (electroencephalography) provides brain-mapping data based on the very precise localization of brain wave patterns coming from the parts of the brain actively engaged in the processing of information.

ACKNOWLEDGMENTS

To Malana and Alani Willis, my daughters and my heroes; Norma Aller-hand, a mom who convinced me there were no limits to dreams; Joyce Dudley, the family's first author; my South Coast Writing Project Family, including Sheridan Blau, Rosemary Cabe, and Patent Animals: Jack Phre-aner, Mona Pinon, Joanie Brown, and Elizabeth Grace; Jules Zimmer; and my UCSB Gevirtz Graduate School of Education colleagues. To my Santa Barbara Middle School family of students, parents, faculty, administration, and staff—you make weekdays as much fun as weekends.

None of the words I wrote would have made it to these pages without the encouragement and wisdom of Scott Willis and the sage editing of Deborah Siegel.

In loving memory of my teachers Aunt Ruth Ackerman, Richie Berman, and Sabrina Tuvey.

1

MEMORY, LEARNING, AND TEST-TAKING SUCCESS

The past two decades have provided extraordinary progress in our understanding of the nature of learning. Never before have neuroscience and classroom instruction been so closely linked. Because advances in technology enable us to view the working brain as it learns, educators can now find evidence-based neuroimaging and brain-mapping studies to determine the most effective ways to teach.

Brain Plasticity and Pruning

Learning causes growth of brain cells. For a long time, scientists held a misconception about brain growth: they believed it stopped at birth and was followed by a lifetime of brain cell death. Now we know that although most of the neurons where information is stored are present at birth, there is lifelong growth of the support and connecting cells that enrich the communication between neurons. These dendrites sprout from the arms (axons) or the cell body of the neuron.

Dendrites increase in size and number in response to learned skills, experience, and information. New dendrites grow as branches from frequently activated neurons. This growth is stimulated by proteins called neurotrophins. Nerve growth factor is one of these neurotrophins. Although the brain measurements of neurotrophins are highest during childhood (when the brain's connecting cells are undergoing their greatest growth and development), as students continue to learn, neurotrophin activity is elevated in the brain regions responsible for new learning (Kang, Shelton, Welcher, & Schuman, 1997).

Once these dendrites are formed, the brain's plasticity allows it to reshape and reorganize the networks of dendrite-neuron connections in response to increased or decreased use of these pathways (Giedd et al., 1999).

Examples of brain plasticity have been noted when people repeatedly practice activities controlled by parts of their visual, motor, sensory, or coordination systems for specialized learned activities. Blind people who read Braille have significantly larger somatosensory cortexes, where the sense of touch in their right fingers is processed. Similarly, violin players who use the fingers of their left hands to do the complicated movements along the strings have larger somatosensory regions in the area of their parietal lobe associated with the fingers of the left hand.

A 2004 report in *Nature* found that people who learned how to juggle increased the amount of gray matter in their occipital lobes (visual memory areas). When they stopped practicing the juggling, the new gray matter vanished. A similar structural change appears to occur in people who learn—and then don't practice—a second language. The decrease in connecting dendrites and other supporting brain connecting cells that are not used is called pruning. The loss of native language ability, juggling skills, or learned academic material that is not practiced is the flip side of the brain's growth response to learning. It is the "use it or lose it" phenomenon. The process is called "pruning" because the brain pathways and connections that are used regularly are maintained and "hard-wired," while others are eliminated, or pruned.

Pruning. Just as hedges are pruned to cut off errant shoots that don't communicate with many neighboring leaves, the brain prunes its own inactive cells. By the time we enter adolescence, our brain has chosen most of the final neurons it will keep throughout our adult life based on which cells are used and which are not.

Neurons are pruned when they are not used. Active cells require blood to bring nourishment and clear away waste, but cells that are inactive don't send messages to the circulatory system to send blood. (The brain cells receive circulation not from blood, as seen in the rest of the body, but rather from a colorless, filtered form of blood called cerebral spinal fluid.) This reduced blood flow means that calcium ions accumulate around the cell and are not washed away. This build-up of calcium ions triggers the secretion of the enzyme calpain, which causes cells to self-destruct.

 Gray Matter

To think about pruning in terms of brain cell growth, consider first the astonishing development of the embryonic brain that by week four is producing half a million neurons every minute. During the next several weeks these cells travel to what will become the brain and begin to form branching axons and dendrites. The synaptic junctions that are present at each connection between neuron, dendrite, or axon reach a maximum development rate of two million per second. This plethora of neurons and neuronal connections is pruned in the last few weeks before birth. The orphaned neurons that did not form connections with neighboring cells die off, and only the neurons that are in networks remain and become differentiated into circuits with specific functions (Sowell, Peterson, & Thompson, 2003).

After birth, the brain's gray matter has another growth spurt, with increased gray matter and connections reaching a maximum density at about age 11. This growth is followed by another pruning phase (Seeman, 1999), when unused and unnecessary memory circuits are broken down. If this second pruning phase did not take place, there would be too many crowded circuits in the brain for it to be efficient—just as a computer with lots of data would take longer to turn on because all the data must be activated before the computer can be used.

The more ways something is learned, the more memory pathways are built. This brain research discovery is part of the reason for the current notion that stimulating the growth of more dendrites and synaptic connections is one of the best things teachers can learn to do for the brains of their students.

When children are between the ages of 6 and 12, their neurons grow more and more synapses that serve as new pathways for nerve signals. This thickening of gray matter (the branching dendrites of the neurons and the synaptic connections they form) is accompanied by thickening in the brain's white matter (fatty myelin sheaths that insulate the axons carrying information away from the neuron and making the nerve-signal transmissions faster and more efficient). As the brain becomes more efficient, the less-used circuits are pruned away, but the most frequently used connections become thicker, with more myelin coating making them more efficient (Guild, 2004).

Helping Students Grow More Brain Connections

In the classroom, the more ways the material to be learned is introduced to the brain and reviewed, the more dendritic pathways of access will be created. There will be more synaptic cell-to-cell bridges, and these pathways will be used more often, become stronger, and remain safe from pruning.

For example, offering the information visually will set up a connection with the occipital lobes (the posterior lobes of the brain that process optical input). Subsequently or simultaneously having students *hear* the information will hook up a dendritic circuit with the temporal lobes (the lobes on the sides of the brain that process auditory input and play an important role in the regulation of emotion and memory processing). This duplication results in greater opportunity for future cues to prompt the brain access to this stored information.

Multiple stimulations mean better memory. The more regions of the brain that store data about a subject, the more interconnection there is. This redundancy means students will have more opportunities to pull up all those related bits of data from their multiple storage areas in response to a single cue. This cross-referencing of data strengthens the data into something we've learned rather than just memorized.

For example, when we learn about our cars, we store the information in brain association areas under multiple categories that relate to the context with which new information about cars is learned. When we see a car, it goes into the visual image cortex. When we see the word C-A-R spelled out, that information goes into a language-association region. After learning about the internal combustion engine, the association is made with "jet and rocket engines are also powered by internal combustion." Later we build associational memories with the cars we've grown up with.

Because the information about cars is stored in multiple brain areas, and cross-referencing occurs among these areas when we think about cars, connecting networks of dendrites sprout among these memory storage areas. This circuitry permits multiple cues or stimuli to call forth all our car knowledge instantaneously. Just seeing the word "car" will put our recall systems online to provide all the stored data we have connected pertaining to cars. We may not need all that information, but because the associations activate these circuits, any of the stored information that we do need will be rapidly and efficiently accessible.

That is the reason for teaching important material through multiple learning pathways such as several senses (hearing, seeing, touching) as well as through several subjects (cross-curricular topics).

From enriched cages to enriched classrooms and curriculum. Even before plasticity was fully understood, neuroimaging laboratory research demonstrated how growing brains are physically shaped by experience. The brain sizes and weights of rats reared in standard cages were compared with those that lived in enriched cages (where the rats had more objects that they could manipulate). The rats reared in enriched environments had brains that were larger and heavier. Their dendrites, neural pathways, and connections were much longer and more complex, and the pathways branched out to more areas of their brains.

Chimpanzees living in enriched environments with stable social communities showed an increase in dendrite sprouting and synaptic connections in proportion to their increased ability to perform complex memory tasks, such as learning their way around a new maze. They also appeared to interact more positively with members of their group and to work more tenaciously on tasks and problems.

If a few pieces of metal in a rat cage and a stable community of chimps can do all that, think what educators can do in classrooms and with curriculum. In addition, building a supportive social classroom community, with enriched input from the environment, will result in more brain pathways and greater speed and efficiency of brain signals.

Educators as Memory Enhancers, Not Just Information Dispensers

There are many classifications of the types of memory, and the one presented here is a composite of several existing ones. From the most basic awareness of our environment, our memory skills progress to rote memory, working (short-term) memory, patterning and connections to relational memory, and ultimately, long-term memory storage.

Rote memory is unfortunately the most commonly required memory task for students in primary and secondary school. This type of learning involves "memorizing," and soon forgetting, facts that are often of little primary interest or emotional value to the student, such as a list of vocabulary words. Facts that are memorized by rehearsing over and over often don't have obvious or engaging patterns or connections. With nothing to give them context or relationship to each other or to the students' lives, these facts are stored in remoter areas of the brain. These isolated bits are more difficult to locate later because there are few nerve pathways leading to these remote storage systems.

Brain-based strategies can be used to reduce the amount of rote memorization required, and what remains can be less tedious because these strategies help students access and use more effective types of memory storage and retrieval.

The goal of research-based education is to structure lessons to ultimately rely less on inefficient and tedious rote memory. Helping students access and use more effective types of memory storage and retrieval will literally change their brains.

Working memory, or short-term memory, involves the ability to hold and manipulate information for use in the immediate future. Information is held in working memory for only about 20 minutes. The challenge students face is to move information from their working memories into their long-term memories. If they don't do this in about 20 minutes, that information can be lost. (Think about the last time someone gave you driving directions that seemed so clear when you heard them, but were lost to you once you made the second right turn.) To keep this newly learned material from slipping away, it needs to enter the network of the brain's wiring. Students can retain the new information by activating their previously learned knowledge that relates to the new material. This prior knowledge exists in stored loops of brain cell connections (circuits of neurons connected by branching axons and dendrites that carry the information as electrochemical signals). Effective teaching uses strategies to help students recognize patterns and then make the connections required to process the new working memories so they can travel into the brain's long-term storage areas.

Gray Matter

Although it is commonly believed that brain cell growth stops after age 20, that is not completely true. New connecting cells, called dendrites, can be formed throughout life. It is true that the neurons where memory storage takes place are not replenished; however, their extensions, these dendrites, continue to sprout and connect and form new circuits with other dendrites throughout life (Martin & Morris, 2002). These neural networks, similar to electric circuitry, are the roadways that connect various parts of the brain. Just like traffic flow in a busy city, the more alternative pathways there are to connect with a memory, the more efficiently the traffic will flow, and the more rapidly that memory will be retrieved when needed.

After repeated practice, working memories are set down as permanent neuronal circuits of axons and dendrites ready to be activated when the information is needed. When a memory has been recalled often, its neuronal circuits are highly developed because of their repeated activation. A phrase that describes this construction of connections based on repeated association of one piece of information with another is "Cells that fire together, wire together." When neurons fire in sync with one another, they are more likely to form new connections. As the connections grow stronger by repeated stimulation, a given neuron becomes more likely to trigger another connected neuron (Chugani, 1998).

Like an exercised muscle, these circuits then become more efficient and easier to access and activate. Practice results in repeated stimulation of the memory circuit. Like hikers along a trail who eventually carve out a depression in the road, repeated practice stimulates cells in the memory circuit so that the circuit is reinforced and becomes stronger. This means it can be quickly turned from off to on, and switched on through a variety of cues coming in from the senses.

Recall the first few times you learned and practiced a new computer process, such as making a Web page or using e-mail. At first you may have followed step-by-step written or verbal instructions. You possibly needed to rely on those instructions multiple times as you repeated the task, until one day, the process became automatic and you could even carry on a conversation while doing the job. That working memory was embedded by repetition into long-term memory, but it still needed periodic repetition for it to remain in your active memory bank and not gradually fade from disuse. Even if it did fade when you were away from your computer during summer vacation, however, the neuronal circuit or brain cell network that was created was still physically present in your brain, just like that hiking trail under the winter's snow. It was just in storage, like data taken off your computer desktop and put into the hard drive, and it took less time to refresh it than it did to learn it the first time.

 Gray Matter

A review of the anatomy of the brain provides background for interpreting brain-based research about the memory storage and retrieval process. The brain is divided into lobes, each with many functions, each interconnecting to the other lobes through nerve pathways or circuits. For example, areas in the left frontal lobe and both temporal lobes are integral in executive attention—alerting the rest of the brain to pay attention or respond to stimuli. In the context of learning, the stimuli are the bits of sensory information students see (through their eyes or by visualization), hear, feel, smell, touch, or experience through movement

Even more specialized brain regions that are most active during the moments when new information is actively learned and stored have been revealed through neuroimaging and brain mapping. First, there are the somatosensory cortex areas, one in each brain lobe, where input from each individual sense (hearing, touch, taste, vision, and smell) is received and then classified or identified by comparing it with previously stored data. Next in the sequence of memory storage are the reticular activating system (alerting the brain to sensory input that sense receptors in the body send up the spinal cord) and the limbic system, comprised of parts of the temporal lobe, the hippocampus (damage to the hippocampus can result in anterograde amnesia, an inability to form new memories), the amygdala, and the prefrontal cortex (Bliss & Collinridge, 1993).

Learning promotes learning. Engaging in the process of learning actually increases one's capacity to learn. Each time a student participates in any endeavor, a certain number of neurons are activated. When the action is repeated, such as when performing a follow-up science lab experiment or rehearsing a song, or when the information is repeated in subsequent curriculum, these same neurons respond again. The more times one repeats an action or recalls the information, the more dendrites sprout to connect new memories to old, and the more efficient the brain becomes in its ability to retrieve that memory or repeat that action.

Eventually, just triggering the beginning of the sequence results in the remaining pieces falling into place. This repetition-based sequencing is how you are able to do many daily activities almost without having to think about them, such as touch-typing or driving a car. The reason for this ability goes back to the construction and strengthening of those memory pathways in the brain.

Very few educators resort to having students learn only by rote memorization or limit instruction to only drill-and-kill worksheets day after day in hopes of imprinting material in students' brains. Teachers know from their own teaching experience how briefly that material remains accessible to students. Many teachers can recall occasions when they accidentally gave students a spelling list or math worksheet they had already completed, and the relatively large number of students who *didn't* instantly recognize that it was the identical work they did only a few weeks, or even days, before.

Now there are more ways to help students process information from lessons so it travels beyond temporary working memory and into memory storage. These strategies keep students interested in what they are learning. These lessons activate multiple senses and connect new information to multiple brain pathways into the memory storage areas. Successful brain-based teaching builds more connections and stronger circuits. Students will have more roadways to carry new information into their memory storage region and to carry out the stored knowledge when it is needed.

 Gray Matter

Brain-mapping techniques allow scientists to track which parts of the brain are active when a person is processing information. The levels of activation in particular brain regions determine which facts and events will be remembered. Functional magnetic resonance imaging (fMRI) allows scientists a view of brain activity over time. In one study focusing on visual memories, subjects were placed under fMRI and then shown a series of pictures. The researchers found that activity levels in the right prefrontal cortex and a specific area of the hippocampus correlated with how well a particular visual experience was encoded and how well it was remembered (Brewer, Zhao, Desmond, Glover, & Gabrieli, 1998).

A study led by Dr. Anthony Wagner (1998) when he was at Harvard Medical School focused on verbal memory. Subjects were asked to analyze words either by their meaning (whether the concept was abstract or concrete) or by their appearance (whether the word was in uppercase or lowercase letters). Activity levels in the prefrontal cortex (but this time on the left, where the Broca's language center is for more than 90 percent of all people) and the same parahippocampal area again predicted which words were remembered in subsequent tests. Furthermore, they discovered that words were much more likely to be remembered when subjects concentrated on the meaning of the words rather than on their appearance (Wagner et al., 1998).

This is an example of how neuroimaging can directly give evidence of the type of memory strategy that works best for the information to be memorized. It also adds evidence to the biological theory that more complex cognition (student-active learning) increases memory retention.

Build stronger memory circuits. Some of the strategies suggested by neuroimaging are ones that have students personalize information to be learned, thereby further activating the areas of the brain that help form memories. Others encourage students to connect with the information with as many senses as possible. They can visualize an electron orbiting the nucleus of an atom, mimic the buzz of electricity as it whizzes by, or feel a tingling associated with the electron's negative charge by rubbing a balloon against their arm and feeling their hair move. If they then draw a sketch of their visualizations and verbally communicate them to partners, or write about them in their own words, multiple brain pathways will be stimulated to enter long-term memory because they have personalized and interacted with the information.

Stimulate Their Senses

The brain may appear to be a tangled bundle of miles of nerve cell connections, but these bundles are in fact organized. From brain mapping we know that predictable tiny regions of the brain are where specific cognitive activities take place. Similarly, imaging has shown us that each of these locations is fed data from brain centers that collect information from the senses and emotions. When students build their working memories through a variety of activities, they are stimulating multiple sensory intake centers in their brains. Their brains develop multiple pathways leading to the same memory storage destination. By stimulating several senses with the information, more brain connections are available when students need to recall that memory later on. This means that the memory can be retrieved by more than one type of cue. If the learned information was taught with visual and auditory associations, it can be recalled by the students using either their sound or visual memory.

My teachers allowed me the exhilaration of my own discovery.
~ Robert Oppenheimer, on how he came to be a nuclear physicist

Surprise

Our brains are structured to remember novel events that are unexpected. Back to basic survival, success is often based on our ability to sense a cause and predict the effect. For example, we get out of the way when we see something being dropped from a roof above us because we predict the possibility of injury from the falling object. Because our brains are encoded to make and respond to predictions, they are particularly stimulated when they predict one effect and experience a different one.

Use surprise to bring students' brains to attention. Consider employing the technique of surprise to light up students' brains and illuminate the pathways to memory storage. Starting a lesson with an unanticipated demonstration or having something new or unusual in a classroom will spark student attention and curiosity. It can be anything from playing a song as they enter to greeting them in a costume. If students sense novel experiences from demonstrations descriptions, anecdotes, or even the enthusiasm in their teacher's voice, they will be more likely to connect with the information that follows.

To take advantage of their engaged state of mind, students should have opportunities to interact with the information they need to learn. The goal is for them to actively discover, interpret, analyze, process, practice, and discuss the information so it will move beyond working memory and be processed in the frontal lobe regions devoted to executive function.

Teachers don't always have to dialogue with individual students to prompt their being "in the moment" with the information, although that certainly worked well for Socrates. Strategies that can achieve these goals include partner discussions and Think-Pair-Share. Students can write *dend-writes* (a more enticing name for class notes that gives student note-taking more status).

They might add a sketch in their notebooks alongside their comments about the surprise, the new information they learned, and their personal response to it (What did I see/hear/smell? What did I learn?

What surprised me? What do I want to know more about? What did this information remind me of?).

New Ways to Use Available Material

When the lesson is a more passive one, such as students reading a section of a textbook in class, teachers can improvise engaging strategies using resources already accessible. Well-crafted textbooks often include comprehension questions at the end of each chapter. However, in the age of interactive computers and video games, the textbook is not likely to grab students' enthusiastic interest without some help from their teacher. Teachers can select some of the text's more thought-provoking questions, the more open-ended questions that prompt connections to previous experiences or learning, and those that encourage students to consider their personal opinions. Instead of assigning the rather tedious, passive homework task of having students read a question, then search the chapter or their notes for "the right answer," teachers can create classroom opportunities to bring these questions to life.

To stimulate more memory circuits, students can use these chapter questions to interview a partner as if for a television news show. They can sketch an abstract representation in response to a concept question (What would the Big Bang or infinity look like?).

It might seem boring or pointless to students if you ask them to check their own notes for accuracy, but with proper teacher modeling to demonstrate respectful and constructive peer editing, students can read the notes of partners and advise them on what they missed. They are also likely to find information in their partner's notes that they will want to add to their own. After any of these activities, partners can "nominate" their classmate's sketch, notes, or interview comments to be shared with the entire class. When teachers have taken steps to engage students' interest long enough for new information to pass from awareness into working memory, students' brains can take over, and these meaningful patterns and memorable connections will penetrate through the brain circuits to relate to and build upon existing stored memory pathways.

Episodic Memory and Experiential Learning

Decades ago, my high school chemistry teacher slowly released hydrogen sulfide (rotten egg smell) from a hidden container he opened just before we entered his classroom. A few minutes after we took our seats and he began his lecture, a foul odor permeated the classroom, grabbing our attention. We groaned, laughed, and looked around for the offending source. To an outside observer entering our class at that time, we would have appeared unfocused and off-task. However, this demonstration literally led me by the nose to follow his description of the diffusion of gases through other gases. It is likely that during that class I created two or three pathways to the information about gas diffusion that I processed through my senses and ultimately stored in my long-term memory. Since then, that knowledge has been available for me to retrieve by thinking of a rotten egg or by remembering the emotional responses as the class reacted to the odor permeating the room. Once I make the connection, I am able to recall the scientific facts linked to his demonstration.

Event memories, such as the one that was stored that day in my chemistry class, are tied to specific emotionally or physically charged events (strong sensory input) because of the emotional intensity of the events to which they are linked. Because the dramatic event powers its way through the neural pathways of the emotionally pre-activated limbic system into memory storage, the associated hitch-hiking academic information gets pulled along with it. Recollection of the academic material occurs when the emotionally significant event comes to mind, unconsciously or consciously. To remember the lesson, students can cue up the dramatic event to which it is linked.

Can you recall a time when you smelled the perfume a friend or loved one wore, and you remembered other details about that person? Perhaps upon hearing an old song, you've recalled dancing to it years before? You can probably visualize where you were when you heard the World Trade Center had been hit. When you think of that event, you probably remember other details of your environment at that moment. Similarly, experiential learning that stimulates multiple senses in students, such as hands-on discovery science, is not only the most engaging, but also the most likely to be stored as long-term memories. Because each of the senses has a separate storage area in the brain, multisensory input results in duplicated storage and can be retrieved by a variety of stimuli. With strategies that engage the senses, students "become" the knowledge by interacting with it. As a result, a new memory that might otherwise be forgotten is linked to a sensation, a movement, or an emotion, and therefore it travels into the memory storage along more than one pathway. This redundancy of pathways means greater memory retention and recall.

Hands-on experiential learning activities are by nature multi-sensory. They actually stimulate two memory systems in separate brain regions that are seen networked together, resulting in powerful cross-referencing on PET scans (Andreason et al., 1999). These activities teach information that is specifically structured into the lesson —factual information such as the process of photosynthesis. That is semantic memory. In addition, there are episodic or event memories stored, such as the sensory input from touching, seeing, measuring, and investigating the plant. Because hands-on activities target both memory systems, there is greater likelihood of retention and less need for inefficient rote memory.

It is not, nor should it be, an educator's role to turn the classroom into a video arcade. We don't want students to be primarily motivated by the external rewards of bells and whistles. An ideal event-memory lesson would be one where students' brains are stimulated by their participation in a challenging and engaging student-centered activity that simultaneously activates multiple sensory systems and executive functions as they strive to make sense of experience. The goal is to provide experiences that enable students to interact with knowledge in ways that arouse their physical senses and positive emotions, or to connect the new information with their past experiences and interests.

Educators can supercharge material to be learned by relating it to students' senses and experiences, and these connections intensify their memory building. This process of connecting new information to related experiences or memories is aptly named relational memory.

Relational Memory—Lighting the Pathways

Learning consists of reinforcing the connections between neurons. Relational memory takes place when students learn something that adds to what they have already mastered; they engage or expand on "maps" already present in the brain. This process engages more executive functions as students' brains scan their stored memory banks seeking relationships that help them put new connections in context.

 Gray Matter

Any new information or learning must enter the brain through one or more of the senses (hearing, seeing or visualizing, touching, tasting, smelling, and emotionally feeling). First, the information is decoded by the sense-specific receptors of the body. From there the information travels through the nerves in the skin or body to the spinal cord and up through the reticular activating system to the specialized part of the brain that receives input from the particular senses.

If all goes well, the information is then carried to the limbic system. After first entering the hippocampus, messages are sent to the prefrontal lobe storage areas, association region, and executive function regions to reactivate any potentially related memories stored there. If previously stored, related memories can be activated and sent to the hippocampus and nearby regions of the temporal lobe, where they are connected to the new information to build relational memories. The brain then makes the conscious connections between these stored memories and the new information, and forms a new integrated memory for storage in the frontal lobe. This relating function of the hippocampus is so critical to the process of creating memories that when the hippocampus is severely damaged, the individual can lose the ability to form new memories.

Patterns are paths for memories to follow. How does relational memory apply to teaching? We already know that rote memory is inefficient, but now there is visible evidence to encourage helping students make connections and see patterns.

Patterning is the process whereby the brain perceives and generates patterns by relating new with previously learned material or chunking material into pattern systems it has used before. Education is about increasing the patterns that students can use, recognize, and communicate. As the ability to see and work with patterns expands, the executive functions are enhanced. Whenever new material is presented in such a way that students see relationships, they generate greater brain cell activity (forming new neural connections) and achieve more successful long-term memory storage and retrieval.

Graphic Organizers

Graphic organizers help students see relationships and pattern new information for memory storage. They are one of the most nourishing of all "dendrite sprout foods" to nurture students' brain growth.

The more educators add the science of teaching to their individual styles and skills, the less students will need to rely on the inefficient and unpleasant process of rote memorization. Graphic organizers are a creative alternative to rote memorization because they enable students to make connections, see patterns, access previously stored related memories, and expand upon existing memory circuitry.

Graphic organizers coincide with the brain's style of patterning. For memory capture to occur, there must first be encoding (the initial processing of the information entering from the senses). If this information is to reach the final stage of enduring memory retention in long-term memory, there must be a process of consolidation and storage, where the otherwise transiently encoded event or information is patterned into a more enduring form (Koutstaal et al., 1997).

Graphic organizers promote this more enduring patterning because material is presented in ways that stimulate students' brains to create meaningful and relevant connections to previously stored memories. They can make associations, discover patterns, sort information, and store the new data as relational memories and then long-term memories (see Figure 1).

Figure 1

Sample Instructions for a Student-Generated Graphic Organizer

1. You will create a graphic organizer with evidence to support the following generalization: *Sleeping 8 to 10 hours each night is good for middle school students.*
2. First, put the generalization in the center of the graphic organizer page.
3. For each fact that you select to support the generalization, include a visual symbol. It can be a picture you draw, a symbol, or clip art.
4. Use at least three colors.
5. Include at least four supporting facts.

Information taught in patterns can be as simple as presenting material in chunked format. Because the working memory has a capacity for immediate recall limited to from five to nine pieces of unrelated items, if information is separated into chunks, students can remember it more successfully. Just as phone numbers and social security numbers are divided into chunks of three or four, information—from biologic genus-species names to states and capitals—can be chunked into groupings of three or four, ideally with some commonality that relates them.

When graphic organizers help students cluster information, the process enhances the brain's natural tendency to construct meaning by forming patterns. The best graphic organizers engage the students' imaginations and positive emotions in a creative process whereby they recognize, sort, and discover patterns for themselves. In addition, the use of graphic organizers to connect information in meaningful relationships allows students time for reflecting about the information. The result is that they can ultimately go beyond regurgitating rote memorization to the higher cognitive process of using the information in significant ways. The relational memories they store will be available for critical thinking and other executive functions to use for meaningful problem solving.

Graphic organizers are intrinsically engaging, as they require students to interpret and interact with the material. When students create their own categories (personal relevance) the connection is increased. If they are provided a framework for their organizers, it is helpful if they understand the logic of the structure they are given.

When students make this connection of new to previously stored memories, they experience the sentiment described in the quote from Doris Lessing, "That is what learning is. You suddenly understand something you've understood all your life, but in a new way."

Maintaining Alertness and Improving Memory Retrieval

Teachers develop the ability to read their students' body language, and this skill can let them know when it is time for brain breaks ("synnaps") or altering their mode of instruction. Alertness and memory retrieval increase with more varied modes of instruction of the same material, so one-lesson-fits-all formats should be avoided. Differentiated instruction is one way to gear instruction toward a different type of intelligence each time the lesson is retaught. The better textbooks provide suggestions for these alternative teaching approaches.

Flashbulb memories. As described previously, powerful emotional events are also retrieval-building tools. These flashbulb memories, such as the destruction of the Twin Towers or the Challenger or Colombia blowing up, result in powerful association memories such as what we were doing at the time we heard or saw the event.

These vivid, photographic memories of a lesson punctuated with positive visual and emotional content can include student dramatization in a lesson, pantomiming a vocabulary word, acting out a history skit, or role-playing a conversation in a foreign language. (Students will also benefit from the physical movement and change these activities provide). For these purposes I keep a box of costumes, especially hats, in my classroom at the ready for lessons well suited for dramatization.

Along these same lines, students benefit by being personally involved in the subject material with techniques such as hands-on manipulatives, field experience, experimentation, or even whole body movement (total physical response) to potentiate the implantation of the new information into memory and improve retrieval later. Some specific activities include the following:

1. Multiple forms of review, such as concept maps to provide framework for retrieval.

2. Visual imagery: Visualize the historical event using words or pictures on paper.

3. Personal relevance: Tie the information to their lives. Think, write about the connection, and share with a partner.

4. Produce a product or make models.

5. Role-play or pantomime.

Once the information is successfully retrieved, it still needs to be reviewed between four and seven times to ensure retention. Review beyond a single perfect response permits the new neural networks to fire correctly more than once. The more they fire, the easier it is to access and retrieve the information later.

The best learning occurs when students are given opportunities to develop their capacities to think, interpret, and become engaged in subject matter. It therefore behooves educators to become mentors not only of the subject matter taught, but also of the memory and retention process. Brain-based research has yielded the strategies that improve students' receiving, encoding, storing, and retrieving of information, but there is an emotional aspect to consider as well. These next strategies strive to

- Keep student anxiety and stress low.
- Punctuate lessons with attention-grabbing moments.
- Improve student memory and retention by making connections to previously learned material, personal experience, and positive emotional states.
- Enrich lessons with multisensory input.
- Access multiple intelligence strategies authentically connected to the material.

Punch Up Lessons

When the 6th grade students entered Ms. Patterson's class one late October morning, the room was darkened, with candlelight the only illumination. Desks were pushed to the sides, a few blankets were spread on the floor, and a "director's chair" faced the classroom. Their delight at this haunted setting allayed any fears of their pending oral presentations of scary stories, and because of this novel surprise, they were more attentive than ever before.

One of the reasons the first day of school is exciting for most students is because there is novelty. It can be the new teacher, new classmates, different bulletin board, new textbook, or even a change of view out the classroom window. Enthusiasm is generated when students are presented with novelty and find creative ways to explore or connect with the new material and are inspired by it. If teachers can generate this awe and sense of wonder, students will be pulled into the lesson and want to connect with the information in a meaningful way.

Brains search for meaning to successfully encode new information. Students' attention must be engaged before the new information can be perceived, encoded, and patterned. Novelty, humor, and surprise in lessons expedite students' attentive focus, and the use of these strategies results in more successful encoding of data into the memory circuits (Koutstaal et al., 1997).

Interactive strategies that incorporate novelty and engage attention can include quiz show formats. New and changing match-game puzzles at workstations with colored stickers or humorous sketches will engage students' attention. Then students can perform the patterning task of connecting one fact to another. This match-game process can be applied to words and their definitions or to two sides of math or science equations. Even changing where students sit brings freshness to their classroom experience.

Lessons don't all have to involve elaborate surprises to be motivating. In planning ways to punch up the memory links for the material taught, teachers can engage students' interest through student-centered lessons. Something as simple as a mirror can personalize a learning activity—ask the students to look in the mirror and respond to a writing prompt such as, "What will the person in the mirror do to make the world a better place?" or "What will the person in the mirror do if he or she hears a racial slur?" Even with a large class, strategies that connect individual students with the material in personal ways are key to keeping students tuned in and their brains turned on.

Personal Meaning

As noted previously, a student must care about new information or consider it important for it to go through the limbic system expeditiously, form new synaptic connections, and be stored as a long-term memory. In other words, memories with personal meaning are most likely to become relational and long-term memories available for later retrieval. Student-centered learning can lead to mastery, because the lesson has personal meaning that they can see has the potential to increase their success and skill in achieving something they care about.

Hooks to connect. Learning should and can be exciting when students relate new information to past experiences. This connecting lets them personalize the learning and increases opportunities for its placement in the relational memory system. If they don't have any links to hook into, teachers can start them off with scaffolding through structured outlines or graphic organizers that they can fill in after they participate in an active learning experience. They can then personalize the information by thinking of ways in which they might use it in future careers or hobbies.

This same positive neural circuit connecting occurs when the lesson is associated with a positive emotional experience. The positive emotional experience can be the result of feelings of accomplishment, pleasant social interactions with classmates or the teacher, or specific acknowledgment and praise. This emotional connection is particularly applicable during adolescence. The influences of emotions and hormones are greatest during the elementary and middle school years, making these years a particularly significant time to use teaching strategies that make the most of the heightened emotional state of students.

An example would be to help students reach a state of excited interest and emotional comfort by introducing the material in association with something that the class always enjoys. This association can be a lesson that starts out in the playing field or one that begins with a treat such as popcorn. For example, a new class literature book is sometimes introduced by having students read the first few pages aloud using the "popcorn" or "jump in anytime" read-aloud technique. (In popcorn reading, students take turns reading aloud, but instead of alternating pages or paragraphs, a reader pops in anytime, even in mid-sentence. This reading technique is useful to keep the students following the text while listening to others reading because they must be following the words carefully to pop in.) Before introducing "popcorn reading" you can give out or even pop some popcorn to demonstrate why the technique is called "popcorn." By associating the lesson with a positive emotional memory, the academic memory will be linked and related to the positive emotional memory.

Cross-curricular relational memory building. Learning related material across the curriculum involves activities that increase the connections between different areas of the brain where related information is stored. When students investigate topics creatively with thematic, interdisciplinary approaches, they learn patterns and skills, not just facts. When subjects are interrelated, they are more easily recalled and there is less need for memorization, because higher levels of thinking have been stimulated and there are increased numbers of pathways by which information can travel in and out of long-term memory banks.

Visualization. Visualization is another way for students to create personal connections to the material. After first modeling and describing a visualization of one's own, such as what the teacher pictures when thinking of a sunrise during the fall equinox at the North Pole (which direction are you looking in and at what time of day) and frontloading students with factual information, students are then asked to visualize the science they are learning about, such as the Big Bang that may have occurred at the birth of the universe.

After giving imagination free rein, more of their brains can be engaged if the students put their visualization into words, diagrams, or pictures. They can describe their images to each other, write them in words, or draw sketches. Just as athletes may visualize a move before they execute it, students can be encouraged to visualize a biological process or historical event as it is explained in class. When they draw diagrams, create models, and engage their sight, hearing, smell, touch, or movement, they are making connections between the new information and something they already know. They are engaging multiple brain pathways and increasing the likelihood of memory storage and effective retrieval.

The more bizarre the visual image, the more memorable it becomes. Modeling becomes important here to show them how their teacher pictures a *high* hangman's gallows, built with a right angle, with a *pot in* a *noose* hanging from it, to remember the word and position of the *hy-pot-en-use* in a right triangle. This visualization process can include humor, creativity, pleasure, and self-satisfaction. All of these predispose the limbic system to add emotional power as it passes the image and the attached concept into long-term memory storage. In addition to generating mental images, if kinesthetic activity can be incorporated, the student has at least two different memory circuits activated.

I have used visual images, accompanied by a sketch on the board, for unfamiliar terms, but two that always elicit groans and giggles are so well remembered that new students come to my class asking when I'm going to teach them about polygons and the rhombus. Similarly, former students come back and tell me they never forgot those terms. For the explanation of open versus closed polygons, I draw a closed, multisided polygon with a bird inside. I then open the polygon by erasing one of the sides. I next erase the bird and say, "When the polygon is open, *Polly* is *gone.*" I'm glad I can't hear your groan or I might not proceed with the rhombus. I draw a square and tell the students that one day a new, inexperienced bus driver was on the road and hit the square. I then sketch the square after it was struck by this WRONG BUS—it tilts to the side and becomes a *"rong-bus"* or a rhombus. After the groans, I have them stand like squares and imagine that the wrong bus taps them, so they tilt a bit and turn into human rhombus-like structures.

If I am short of lesson time for vocabulary words, I might act them out myself and have students select the word from a list on the board that matches my pantomime. Other times I ask them to make a physical response that reminds them of the word. I have a great class photo that was taken when I asked them all to show me a "haughty" expression, after first prompting them that it might be the expression a rude king or queen might make after being served tea from a dirty cup by an unwashed servant.

Even with highly conceptual learning, such as political systems or philosophy, if the students can actively do something with the new information, they can ultimately own it and store it in permanent memory. The more abstract the information, the more creative teachers need to be to help students relate the material to personal experiences or consider its practical or future applications.

For example, historical events can be personalized by turning them into ethical dilemmas students might face today. Students can experience firsthand the dilemmas of the non-Jews during the Holocaust who struggled with the risks to their own families in hiding Jews from Nazis. Follow a lesson about those events with a question relating that ethical dilemma to one that could happen today. "What if your neighbor was hurting his dog and you saw him do it again and again. What if he saw you watching him and told you he would poison your dog if you reported him. What would you do? How would you feel?" When children consider how they would respond, the history takes on personal meaning and becomes relational memory.

Limbic System Stimulation—Not Too Hot, Not Too Cold, but Just Right

The amygdala is part of the limbic system in the temporal lobe. It was first believed to function as a brain center for responding only to anxiety and fear. Indeed, when the amygdala senses threat, it becomes overactivated (high metabolic activity as seen by greatly increased radioactive glucose and oxygen use in the amygdala region on a PET scan). In students, these neuroimaging findings are seen when they feel helpless and anxious. When the amygdala is in this state of stress, fear, or anxiety-induced overactivation, new information coming through the sensory intake areas of the brain cannot pass through the amygdala to gain access to the memory circuits.

More recent studies have found that the amygdala also is stimulated, but to a lesser degree of metabolic activity, when students are in a positive emotional state with feelings of contentment, joy, play, and a comfortable, but stimulating, amount of challenge.

During these emotional states, neuroimaging shows metabolic states of low-level stimulation in the amygdala. Students tested under these conditions show better working memory, improved verbal fluency, better episodic memory for events, and more flexible thinking yielding creative ideas for problem solving. They even show more positive social behaviors—helpfulness, sociability, focus, patience, and other higher-order executive function and decision-making abilities.

Subsequent research revealed that after presentation of pleasurable, comforting, positively reinforcing, intrinsically motivating stimuli, the amygdala could be moderately stimulated or warmed up to the alert state that actually facilitates active processing and neuronal transport of information. This represents the actual neuroimaging visualization of what has been called the affective filter—an emotional state of stress in students during which they are not responsive to processing, learning, and storing new information. This represents objective physical evidence that during periods of high stress, new learning just doesn't get in to the information processing centers of the brain.

To prevent overactivation of the amygdala, protect students from aversive experiences that would block the passage of new information into long-term memory. The type of stressful experiences that can result in amygdala blockage include calling out students' failing test grades aloud as exams are returned, teaching a lesson in a language that students don't understand without using TPR (total physical response, with gesturing, pointing to objects, pantomime, and other techniques to give them the information they need), or ignoring hands raised with questions without telling the students that you will get to their questions within a few minutes after you finish making your point. (Once students don't understand a part of a process, such as a step in a math calculation, it is stressful to hear the teacher continue on while they are lost. If they are assured that their questions will soon be answered, they don't overstress.) In general the type of stress that is overpowering is a helplessness connected to hopelessness.

 Gray Matter

PET scans show how information coming from the sensory receptor areas of the brain must travel through the amygdala to get into the hippocampus, from where it can be sent to the executive function and long-term memory storage areas in the frontal lobe. These scans demonstrate that when the amygdala is in its highly metabolic state of hyperstimulation from stress, these pathways leading to memory storage are blocked. When they are blocked by the flooded amygdala, the scans demonstrate a lack of metabolic activity in the centers of reasoning and long-term memory. In other words, when the limbic system, particularly the amygdala, is hyperstimulated by high stress, it becomes flooded by so much neural metabolic activity that new memories cannot pass through it to memory storage and reasoning parts of the brain.

The research represents the actual neuroimaging visualization of what has been called the affective filter—an emotional state of stress in students during which they are not responsive to processing, learning, and storing new information.

However, as important as it is to avoid overactivation of the amygdala, it is also important to provide mild-to-moderate challenge to stimulate authentic curiosity and engagement in lessons so the amygdala, tuned to just the ideal state of activation, can enhance the speed and efficiency of information flowing through into the memory storage areas of the brain. It is just the right balance of these emotional and intellectual opportunities, and the incorporation of students' own interests and curiosity into the lesson, that will motivate them to work toward greater understanding and connection with the material. As students access this pathway with open-ended and student-initiated questioning, they will engage their higher-order executive functions and, with practice, experience the confidence to see themselves as learners with open minds. Educators can help students unlock the gatekeeper (amygdala or affective filter) for sensory data. Once the information can get through the amygdala, it can be linked with students' personal interpretations and teacher-guided meaning. These memories have the best chance of entering long-term memory storage banks.

Syn-*naps*

Every brain needs periodic rests during which neurotransmitters can be replenished and executive function can process the new material. The use of the word *"Syn-naps"* is an example of the use of word play to help build memory. The synapse is the gap between nerve endings where neurotransmitters like dopamine carry information across the space separating the axon extensions of one neuron, from the dendrite that leads to the next neuron on the pathway. The creation of a word like *syn-naps* helps teachers recall that after repeated release of neurotransmitters from a nerve ending, there needs to be a brain rest when the neurotransmitter can be restored to be available for release when the next message comes traveling along the neuronal circuit. These syn-naps are restorative breaks that are as important for successful memory retention as are other elements such as surprise, positive emotional state, sensory memories, and other relational memories. Not only do these "naps" prevent overloading of the circuits and interference with maximal memory storage conditions, but they also help maintain positive emotional states.

If the lesson involves complex material, especially in a lecture mode, syn-naps can be necessary after as little as 15 minutes. When students are entering a state of depletion of neurotransmitters in their synapses, they will become fidgety, distracted, and unfocused. It is best to have students take the brain rest before neurotransmitter depletion occurs and before stress builds up in the amygdala, inhibiting new information intake. If the neurotransmitters are not being replenished as fast as they are being used, or if amygdala hyperactivity is beginning to block new information input, memory efficiency drops rapidly. In this burnout state, new memories can't be stored efficiently.

 Gray Matter

Syn-*naps* are also necessary to replenish neurotransmitters. Neurotransmitters, such as the amino acids serotonin, tryptophan, and dopamine, transport information across the synapses. (Synapses are microscopic gaps between nerve cells where information cannot be carried in the electrical state it is in when it travels down the nerve. It must travel across the synaptic gap attached to a chemical neurotransmitter, like a passenger on a boat crossing a river.)

These neurotransmitters are released on one side of the synaptic gap and float across the synaptic space to the next nerve cell, where they hook on to specialized receptors. When this hook-up takes place, the electrical transmission down that next nerve in the circuit nerve is reactivated. When neurotransmitters are depleted by too much information traveling through a nerve circuit without a break, the speed of transmission along the nerve slows down to a less efficient level. When this happens, information processing takes longer, leading not only to student frustration, but also to less successful memory storage.

Depleted neurotransmitters rebuild within minutes if the break is taken before complete meltdown, but their rebuilding takes longer if they are severely depleted. It is ideal to prevent burnout by planning brain rests before students display the first signs of glazed expressions or distraction. If these overload/depletion times are anticipated before they occur, and students have a break before that point, the topic about which they were learning will not be linked or negatively reinforced by their associating feeling bored with that topic when it comes up again.

During these rests, the newly learned material has the opportunity to go from working or short-term memory to relational memory (although it will not become a permanent memory until time and practice follow). The students can start the break with a complete change of pace by moving about the room, drinking water, stretching, singing, dancing, or taking a bathroom break. However, after that transition, it is critical to implement the strategies that have proven most effective in cementing the working memory into relational memory and long-term memory.

After the rest or physical movement is the time to use a student-centered cementing strategy—one that was not used earlier in the lesson. It has been said that we file by similarities and we retrieve by differences, so here is the opportunity for students to identify and discuss similarities and differences. Here are a few techniques:

• Draw Venn diagrams.

• Generate mental images (if not done previously) and think about what other mental pictures come to mind in association with these new ones.

• Create metaphors and analogies.

Analogies, although no longer part of the SAT, remain effective ways for students to conceptualize and thereby interact and connect with instruction by comparing the similarities or differences between two chunks of information. After syn-naps, students can try to create a simile or metaphor that helps them abstract the new material, such as, "Adverbs give more meaning to verbs like acting kindly gives more meaning to a friendship." This analogy-building process is a way of physically structuring the memory circuits, or bringing stored similar memories online to connect with the new information.

Students may benefit from prompts to make analogous connections with questions such as these: In what way was the American Revolution like a baseball strike? How are human hands like bats' wings? How are babies like the new seedlings we are growing? How is mutation-based evolution similar to the TV show *Survivor*?

Greater connections to book reports, history reports, and empirical essays can occur when students use analogies in the form of personal anecdotes that begin the essay and are concluded at the end of the report. This strategy not only connects the student personally with the topic, but is also a compelling way to draw in readers.

Memory is strengthened by insight; when students understand concepts well, it is much easier for them to remember relevant facts. This memory strengthening is what occurs when students use analogies, metaphors, and personal anecdotes to connect new information to their own stored internal graphic organizers—their neuron-dendrite networks.

Repetition and Consolidation

Multiple mechanisms work to maintain stored memory, including recollection, familiarity, and priming. Once the information is remembered correctly and used with executive functions, it still needs to be reviewed on a regular basis, but at gradually lengthening intervals. This repetition, after the first correct response, results in reinforcement of the neuronal connections along the lengths of the axons and dendrites and across the synapses. The more the neural connections are activated by the stimulation that practice brings, the more dendrites grow to strengthen the connections between the neurons.

 Gray Matter

fMRI studies during the learning of a motor movement (in this case learning to play the piano) revealed that during these initial learning stages, a large portion of the brain's motor control region is activated. With practice and improved skill levels, smaller and smaller regions of the brain are activated during the piano playing. In professional musicians, only very tiny regions of the motor cortex are involved in their playing. The conclusion drawn was that because practice makes the neural networks more efficient, it took less brain metabolism to carry out the same activity. The result is that there is freeing up of brain energy and areas to be used for other things (Jancke, 2000).

When the brain perceives information repeated in multiple ways, there is a *priming* process that makes encoding of that information more efficient. That is why writing a vocabulary word in a sentence, hearing classmates read their sentences, and then following the direction to use the word in conversation during that day will result in more successful long-term memory storage and retrieval than just memorizing the definition (Koutstaal et al., 1997).

This varied repetition of the information results in *consolidation of information*. Consolidation of information involves using the most effective strategies to first acquire information and then practice and rehearse it. The best-remembered information is learned through multiple and varied exposures followed by authentic use of the knowledge by processing it through the executive function centers. This executive function processing of new information can be achieved by student-centered or open-ended questions, active problem solving, or connecting the information to real-world situations.

These steps along the way will change the sensory data students are bombarded with into knowledge they will own. These multiple and varied exposures and higher cognitive processing result in more pathways leading to the newly stored information. That means there will be more ways to later access the information for retrieval after it has been stored in the long-term memory centers.

Strategies to Consolidate Learned Material into Long-Term Memory

• Introduce the information when students are engaged, with focused attention.

• Include practice of accurate and precise observation techniques where students learn the information in a meaningful context. Encourage students to repeat information you want them to remember over and over, even in conversation: "Isn't it odious how much chewing gum is on the bottom of some restaurant tables?" "Oh yes, it is even more odious when you have to clean it."

• Use multisensory avenues of exposure to the information that result in multiple connections and relational memory links to existing memory circuits to increase recall and memory storage.

• Create student-centered, personal motivation for learning. For example, if there is math or science that needs to be mastered in the curriculum standards, students can be motivated to learn, even memorize, the basics—algebra, structural geography, physiology, cellular chemistry, aerodynamics, and wave mechanics—to reach their goal of building a model land-water amphibious vehicle.

• Use skilled and practiced observation techniques (on initial exposure and repeated opportunities to observe again as topic of study continues) to make personal connections and discoveries about the material to be learned.

• Have students use the information to answer personally relevant, critical thinking questions or make and support judgments using the new knowledge.

• Pose practical, real-world problems for students to solve using the new knowledge.

• Ask students how they might use the information outside of school. How might it be important in what they are considering as a possible future career? How might it be valuable to their parents' jobs?

Just as personal interest and novel activities generate interest in the big picture of a new topic, these techniques are also valuable in culminating experiences. For example, after we studied the daily life of the early American colonists, we had Colony Day. Students could dress in colonial attire, bring authentic colonial foods, teach the class a colonial game, act in the role of a famous person from colonial times, or demonstrate a craft or professional skill from that era. Students could *choose* their type of participation, and use executive function and the newly acquired knowledge of colonial life to evaluate the best ways to proceed with their plans, plan and prioritize a schedule to prepare for their activity, and predict any problems that might come up. They also had to know their information well enough to respond to high-level peer questioning about the role of their person, food, or activity in colonial society.

Culminating Activities as Memory Cement

• Students make ongoing observations and continually revise and refine their hypotheses. (The basis of my medical training and practice was to carefully observe patients, make a preliminary list of possible diagnoses, then question further, examine, and collect data to narrow and refine my diagnosis. This revising and refining process is actually done by students when they use an Internet search engine such as Google and refine their terms to cull the specific information they need from the thousands of initial references.)

• Students are guided to analyze and compare their own work and the work of experts.

• Students are encouraged to check on facts and details and to test their beliefs and conclusions.

• Students use graphic organizers and activities like KWL. When students connect new information with similar stored knowledge in KWL, this "priming" increases familiarity and therefore improves recall. For example, after studying the word "seatbelt," when shown the word "seat" in word association, the most likely response is "belt."

• Students are asked student-centered, open-ended questions and critical thinking questions to increase depth of understanding. These questions can be prompted by the teacher, but should come from students' personal interest in the information to be learned. Starting with a global initial presentation appealing to their interests, students will want to ask questions to gain more information and make sense of things they see, hear, and read about.

• Students are given multiple exposures to the same or similar information over time. Scaffolding is provided through questions and summarizing activities to confirm that students have learned the facts and strategies needed to be successful in standardized tests and in the future use of the information to serve their needs.

• Students are assessed using authentic assessment; they are evaluated in how they use the material for problem solving, good decision making, creative thinking, making predictions, comparisons (metaphors/analogies), and critical thinking.

• Students use metacognition and reflection to learn from the learning process they engaged in and develop skills to monitor their own future learning.

🧠 **Gray Matter**

Metacognition—knowledge about one's own thoughts and the facts that influence one's thinking and learning—can optimize learning. Despite all the information neuroimaging and brain mapping have yielded about the acquisition of information, some of the best strategies are those that students recognize themselves. Research has demonstrated that optimal learners practice distinct behaviors. After a lesson when students are prompted to recognize a breakthrough success in the learning processing that they experienced that day, they should reflect on what they did right.

So much time is spent focusing on helping students correct their errors and understand their mistakes that there may be little time left to reinforce their successful strategies. When they reflect and discover that on this successful day they took more notes, sat away from distracting classmates, participated more in the discussion, drew a meaningful sketch, enjoyed playing the match game, or made a correct prediction, that metacognition shows them a tool they will use again. It could ultimately become one of the distinct learning behaviors that enhances their competence and confidence and helps them become optimal learners.

Students benefit from multiple opportunities to practice the metacognitive process of making the unconscious conscious. This is time for students to examine their learning experiences and develop this self-awareness. Prompting questions can be used, such as these: What was easy and what was difficult? What worked well and what would you do differently? What did you learn about working in a group? If the student had been doing poorly in a subject and then did higher-quality work on a test, report, or project, he or she might respond to the question, "Why do you think you were so successful this time, and what can you do so you can continue this good work?"

The brain-based techniques already described to enhance memory are geared to increase connectedness through familiarity, personal engagement, and varied repetition and review. When these strategies are used, most of the work to promote long-term memory storage and successful memory retrieval has been done. Because the new material was reinforced through reminders of personal connection at the conclusion of the lesson, and because students were asked open-ended questions about what they found interesting, what they were reminded of, and what they still want to know about, they will be able to take the lesson beyond the classroom door, perhaps even into the lunchroom in a discussion with a classmate, or to the family dinner table.

The list below is a summary of the path to successful memory storage and retention:

1. Information about the world enters the body through the senses.

2. The limbic system and reticular activating system prime the rest of the brain to respond to these sensory inputs.

3. When there is the ideal amount of comfort and stimulation, these activating systems engage memory circuits to an ideal state of readiness. Memory circuits are engaged and ready.

4. Dopamine, adrenaline, and norepinephrine are released in ideal quantities.

5. Information is conducted along memory circuits and connects with previously stored memories and personal experience to form relational memories and patterns.

6. Frontal lobe executive function is activated.

7. The learned, consolidated material is reflected by wisdom as it is retrieved and applied to new situations and future creative problem solving.

Technology as a Memory Tool

Multiple forms of review using different techniques for practicing the same material are of added benefit for memory consolidation, retrieval, and processing through executive function. One reason is that positive reinforcement can be a powerful factor in student learning, and because teachers can't always be there to provide that external reinforcement and reward, technology can help.

Some students don't have Internet access on a readily available computer at home, but most do have this access in computer labs or libraries at school. In addition, many current textbooks in mathematics, history, and other subjects have CD-ROM versions or extensions of the texts or Web pages with interactive activities for students and teachers.

Because much of the computer interactive technology starts in the mathematics field, an example available for trial use is the ALEKS system at *www.K12aleks.com*. This is an example of how a successful interactive computer program can reinforce learning and retention for students. The students are signed into the program by a teacher who can then monitor their time spent, progress, and learning speed, and see not only the concepts they have mastered, but also the concepts that are in their ZPD (Vygotsky's zone of proximal development or readiness). The topics that the student is ready to learn are then presented to them using a pie chart offering a selection of subtopics from which they can select.

One of the most powerful factors in student learning is feedback, because it reinforces neurons in the brain. This ALEKS system gives positive feedback to the students and therefore reinforces neuron circuits in their brains. The reward they receive is authentic because it acknowledges their accomplishments and is directly connected to the learning that just took place or was learned in earlier lessons and tested in a periodic assessment. In the ALEKS system, progress feedback is available to teachers and students at any time and each new lesson starts with a review of the material previously learned.

Well-engineered computer adjuncts can enhance students' memory connections, pathways for access, and retention of the material they learn in the classroom and read in their texts. However, it is up to teachers, administrators, and curriculum teams to evaluate a program's assessment system. Look for a system where periodic assessments review all topic areas of the course. This not only reinforces existing memory, but should also prompt appropriate review when knowledge gaps are revealed. Some computer systems evaluate only the student's recall of the topics taught since the last assessment. Those do not adequately address the long-term memory retrieval. If a student has forgotten things learned earlier in the course, the assessment should recognize and report these gaps when it measures true mastery. The best systems use all of this information when evaluating an individual student's readiness to proceed, and makes those assessments easily accessible and comprehensible for teachers to review.

Once They Leave the Classroom

Most popular magazines and self-help books devote pages to theories on how diet, exercise, and lifestyle affect health and well-being. These factors are so difficult to quantify that it is challenging to make informed decisions. Fortunately, neuroimaging has provided empirical evidence about some of these factors, especially the impact of sleep on memory.

Sleep. During sleep, the cortical executive functioning of the frontal lobes is less active because less sensory input is entering the nervous system. This reduced-activity brain state is just what is needed to allow recently learned material to be rehearsed or repeated, sometimes in dreams. Because sleep is the time when the brain is least distracted by the sensory input bombarding it all day, it can devote a greater portion of its energy (metabolism) to organizing and filing the memories formed during the day.

 Gray Matter

It is known from animal experiments that memory consolidation requires the synthesis of new proteins in the hippocampus and subcortical frontal lobe memory storage areas. These changes appear on fMRI as increased brain oxygen use 24 hours after the information is stored. Thus, it is believed that memories that remain after one day are in the process of being successfully consolidated into neuronal pathways with new dendrites and synaptic connections.

Connections between neurons are sprouted when memories are stored through the growth and interconnections of more dendritic spines. It takes time for these to grow, and that requires not only syn-naps (brain rests), when neurotransmitters such as dopamine are replenished, but also sleep. It is during sleep that the brain reaccumulates the greatest amount of the neurochemicals needed to stimulate dendritic growth.

Memory storage in the brain is most efficient during the longest periods of uninterrupted deep sleep rather than during the "dream sleep" associated with rapid eye movement (REM sleep). This period of deep sleep is the critical time when the brain transforms recent memories into long-term memories by building and extending the dendritic branches. The hard-wiring of information learned during the day results in stored permanent memories.

The more dendrites that branch out from the nerve cells, linking more and more cells together, the more efficiently the brain can recognize similarities between new experiences and already stored ones. This once again illustrates that the more you know, the easier it is to learn.

Growth hormones are especially active during sleep, which is when most of the neurotrophin nerve growth factor stimulation of new dendrite branching takes place. Dendritic branching process is also enhanced by the neurotransmitter serotonin secreted by the brain predominantly between the sixth and eighth hour of sleep. This recognition of the need for sleep has led researchers to test and confirm their predictions that increasing sleep time from six or less to eight hours can increase memory and alertness up to 25 percent (Frank, Issa, & Stryker, 2001).

Sleep helps the brain consolidate and cement new knowledge and experience into memory. This sleep research gives validity to what students have discovered through their own study habits of reviewing notes when they are still alert, rather than just before they fall asleep. Studies suggest that if students review their notes thoroughly and stop and go to sleep when they begin to feel drowsy, the quality and quantity of retained memory is superior to extending the review time any number of hours once drowsiness has set in.

Even when sleep-deprived students catch up on their sleep, their test performance on recently learned information is lowered (Stickgold, 2000). A study of students who received low grades (Cs, Ds, and Fs) revealed that they obtained about 25 minutes less sleep and went to bed an average of 40 minutes later on school nights than students with high grades (As and Bs). Adolescents who slept less than 7 hours reported increased daytime sleepiness, depressed mood, and behavior problems (Wolfson, 1998).

In 2004, Duke University canceled all 8:00 a.m. classes because students weren't getting enough sleep. "They're coming in to see us, and they're ragged," said Assistant Dean Ryan Lombardi. Duke University also plans to offer students individual health assessments for what to eat and how many hours to sleep.

The Future

When brain research on memory and retention is applied to the classroom, it not only drives the learning process, but it also allows educators to energize and enliven the minds of their students. As the research continues to build, it will be up to these professionals to develop and use new strategies that bring the brain-based research to students. That challenge will be a fascinating and exciting one to meet.

2

STRATEGIES TO CAPTIVATE STUDENTS' ATTENTION

All thinking begins with wonder.

~ Socrates

As I sat in the amphitheater lecture hall in one of the older building on the Harvard University campus, that first day of summer school, my mind was miles away from the physics class scheduled to begin momentarily. I was thinking of the beach I would go to after class, the cute boy in front of me with the Grateful Dead tie-dyed shirt, and my pile of dirty laundry that would soon walk away on its own.

The swinging door leading to the lecture area burst open as a man in his late fifties propelled himself into the room sitting on a red wagon, aiming an activated fire extinguisher at the wall. This was Professor Baez on the first morning of class, demonstrating the first law of relativity—that for every action there is an equal and opposite reaction. (Clearly he was an inspiration for his folksinger daughter, Joan Baez.) It wasn't until 30 years later, when I had left my neurology career and had become a teacher trying to get the attention of my students, that I discovered how teachers without red wagons and fire extinguishers could focus student attention. My investigation of brain-based learning research led me to use novelty and excitement through strategies of surprise, unexpected classroom events, dressing in costumes, playing music, showing dynamic videos, putting comic strips or optical illusions on the overhead, and even telling corny jokes, all in the interest of capturing and holding my students' attention.

Before students can make memories or learn, something or someone must capture their attention. Neuroimaging and brain mapping studies have revealed the structural changes in the brain that occur when newly learned information is retained in subcortical storage areas. Although these areas of new memory storage are especially prominent in the subcortical frontal lobes, learning-prompted brain metabolism and the growth of brain cell connections, such as dendrites, can occur in all the lobes of the brain. A recent study demonstrated increased growth in the occipital lobes after subjects learned and practiced juggling.

The preceding chapter noted that memory storage is more efficient when the new information is related to prior knowledge. The more memories in the storage bank, the more neuron circuits there are to connect with the new information. In a similar manner, each time a student focuses attention, the activation of alerting and focusing pathways results in these attention circuits' becoming stronger and more efficient at carrying new data into storage.

Practice or repetition of the process of focusing attention is like exercising a muscle. Neuronal circuits that are activated frequently become more developed because of their repeated stimulation. Practice makes these circuits stronger so they are more efficiently accessed when needed.

 Gray Matter

Awareness is the attention of the moment. The subconscious mind needs to be on automatic pilot to process the enormous amount of information from the world coming in through all the senses. When our brains are working optimally, we recognize some input as familiar but unimportant, and ignore it. We then automatically consider the data needing to be acknowledged at that moment. After brief consideration, the data are either dropped from working memory and disregarded, or selected for further processing. For example, when looking for a particular highway exit, you are aware of the exit signs you pass and pay attention to them momentarily. If an exit is not the one you are looking for, you won't send its name to your working memory bank. Attention becomes not only a matter of focus, but also a matter of correct elimination of inappropriate or unimportant stimuli.

Attention: To Have and to Hold, Set a Positive Emotional Climate

Brain research provides insights into how the brain unconsciously pays attention and tunes in to process information of the moment. When the senses register information, the coded message travels through regions of the brain that can either expedite or block its progress. The thalamus processes the sensory input and determines whether it will be kept in temporary awareness or moved to memory storage. If the input is processed as more than transient awareness, it is passed along to the neurons in the amygdala, where it can be linked to positive emotional cueing and move along to memory storage. If negative emotions have overloaded the amygdala, the affective filter will block passage of the data into memory. Functional MRI (fMRI) scans show that when the limbic system (thalamus, amygdala, hippo-campus, and portions of the frontal lobe) becomes overstimulated by stress-provoking emotion (seen as very high metabolic activity lighting up those limbic brain areas) the information given at that time will not reach the long-term memory centers in the frontal lobe, so these brain centers will not show metabolic activation on PET scans. Conversely, when these gatekeepers of the limbic system are jump-started by positive emotion, more brain activity is seen passing through these portals and lighting up the frontal lobe memory storage centers.

Captivate your audience! Attention is a process of selecting the most relevant information from the mass of sensory input all around us. The *reticular activating system* (RAS) in the lower part of the brain filters all incoming stimuli and makes the decision about what people attend to or ignore. There are three main categories that focus the attention of the RAS and therefore the student. These include physical need, self-made choice, and novelty. It makes sense that physical need be a priority for attention focus because of the powerful survival instinct. Choice also has survival value, because making choices puts the responsibility on the sentient being to evaluate two or more actions to bring about a desired outcome.

The strong reaction to novelty also makes sense, especially for a part of the human brain that is one of the most primitive. Living things need to respond to changes in their environment to survive. We need shelter from sudden storms, new sources of water when streams dry up or plumbing fails, and protection or escape when danger is imminent. A rapid response to newness or novelty is therefore a survival benefit. Because there is so much newness in our students' environment from the visual, auditory, and kinesthetic input all around them (and plugged into their ears from iPods hidden in their backpacks), teachers have the challenge of guiding students to select and focus on the intended information and ignore the rest of the input bombarding their RAS and competing for their attention.

Emphasizing the important information is important because what might seem obvious to an educator may not be as apparent to students. Students benefit from help filtering out some of the distracting environmental stimuli that might interfere with focus on the critical data. Gaining and keeping students' attention will promote information passage from simple momentary awareness to working memory and then to stored long-term memory banks in the subcortical areas of the brain.

One strategy to build anticipation and interest when approaching a required section of curriculum that is critical but could be dull is to build students' curiosity. Posting a sign such as "24 HOURS UNTIL THE FORCE ARRIVES" will certainly stimulate curiosity. The next day, when students hear a lecture about centripetal *force* or the role of the Air *Force* in World War II, they will be in a state of positive anticipation, and that will harness attention.

A medical colleague primes the pump of the residents he teaches by telling them in advance what three or four diseases they will see in the patients they will examine the following day. In that case, knowing what to expect prompts them to read with focus about those illnesses. The information they acquire when they examine and discuss these patients can then be linked to the newly created memory circuits from their reading. The result is greater attention, connection, and memory retention.

Humor and visuals. Just as popular public speakers start their presentations with a joke or funny projected image, successful teachers can use these strategies to captivate student interest. When students enter my math class, I often have optical illusions projected, and they have learned that I want them always to look beyond the obvious. They look forward to coming in and seeing what I'll have up each day.

The human brain and body respond positively to laughter with the release of endorphin, epinephrine (adrenaline), and dopamine, and with increased breathing volume (more oxygen). In addition, the experience of laughing together helps build community. When a lesson starts with humor, there is more alerting, and the subsequent information is attached to the positive emotional event as an event or flashbulb memory.

When color is used in a meaningful way, such as red for arterial blood and blue for venous blood to show amount of oxygen, students pay more attention and remember the information more successfully.

Prime the pump. Students are more engaged when they are interested in the information available for them to learn. Open-ended questions that do not have a single, definite, correct answer and that are student-centered (connected to their interests or experiences) can keep them interested, especially if they receive encouragement for expressing their ideas. Don't permit students to respond immediately. If they are given a reasonable amount of quiet time to think, or if they do a quickwrite or think-pair-share about their opinions of a possible answer, they will be more invested in the topic. For example, "The book *Animal Farm* involves animals as the main characters. Why do you think the author choose to write the story using animals as characters instead of using people?" or, "Why do poets write in verse, and even rhyme, instead of just saying what they want to say in regular paragraphs where they can make their meaning easier to understand?" After this personal involvement with the information, they will be more interested in the lesson because they'll be seeking confirmation of their own opinions or the facts to back them up.

In history, after studying the U.S. Constitution, students can be asked, "How would you create a law that would protect rights of free speech without having the KKK use this law to burn crosses near the homes of black people?" From there, students will be first stimulated, then hopefully a bit frustrated by lack of complete and interpretive knowledge of the Constitution and Bill of Rights. When they finish with a class discussion of the opinions they verbalized with partners or wrote down, they will *want* to learn the information that they *needed* to learn because they became invested in the topic.

Student-centered lessons. PET scans of the same student at different levels of engagement show a hierarchy of brain activity from highest to lowest excitation levels. When the child was reading silently there was the least activity, but as the stimulus was made multisensory there was more activity. When asked to make connections between his life and the story, the activation grew further. Next, when he was told to continue listening to the information in preparation for telling someone about it, there was the greatest amount of brain activity (Sousa, 2000).

It follows that students pay greatest attention when they learn in enriched and varied sensory learning environments with frequent opportunities to connect personally and interpersonally with the material and to feel that it is relevant to their lives.

When possible, engage and maintain students' attention by providing opportunities for them to set their own pace, select the hook that will connect them to the topic, and have some choice in the way they learn the information. An example would be letting a student with an interest in mechanical devices investigate the Revolutionary War period of U.S. history, starting with the weapons used and branching out into the larger topic of availability of raw materials, shipping and transport in Revolutionary times, and how differences in weapons and fighting styles may have mirrored the differences in the philosophies of the British and the colonists. The investigation could begin with books for readers or the Internet for more interactive technology–geared learners. The outcome could include building a battleground simulation, working with a classmate to produce a skit, or dressing in costume and answering the class's questions.

The goal in these student-centered lessons is to increase student engagement by supporting their intrinsic motivation and allowing them to be creative and solve problems while refraining from more directed lecture instruction and from solving problems for them.

Connected minds stay focused. In math, instead of starting with the concept or algorithm students need to learn to do their homework, they can be given a problem that requires that specific knowledge in order to be solved. If students who think they have the answer are not permitted to verbalize their solution, the other students will continue trying to find the solution for themselves. (*The person who thinks, learns.*) Having all students write down their possible solutions gives everyone a chance to be an active participant (especially when they have individual whiteboards they can write on and hold up). When students are a bit frustrated, and *want* to find the solution, perhaps because they think the girl across the room waving her hand knows the answer, they actually want the tool or hint they need to solve the problem on their own. When you build student interest in this way, you change the situation from one of asking students to pay attention to information to which they are not personally connected to one where they are seeking out something they want to know.

The sound in the room will be like popping corn as first one, then another, and another student enthusiastically calls out, "I got it." A consideration with this potentially competitive technique is the student who may not catch on after the hints. They may need preloading (previewing the lesson in advance) or assurance that they will be helped early in the class period when others are working independently.

 Gray Matter

Optimal brain activation occurs when subjects are in positive emotional states or when the material holds personal meaning, connects to their interests, is presented with elements of novelty, or evokes wonder. This is why attentiveness is so closely linked to positive emotional cueing and personal meaning. When there is connection to prior knowledge or positive emotional experience, new information passage through the limbic system will be enhanced. The thalamus will then "decide" to pay attention to the information. If it is then interpreted as having rational meaning, based on previous knowledge, it is linked to existing brain cell networks, which in turn are enlarged, extended, and ultimately strengthened by their reactivation. If there are no emotional or intellectual connections to the new information, and it is not presented in a way that sparks attention, it will be discarded, and attention will be withdrawn.

It is valuable to rotate techniques, lest the unexpected become expected or even tedious. Greeting students at the door with a riddle along with a hello or posing a math problem, the answer to which is the number of the table at which they will sit, gears students up to learn. Giving them an unusual fact or offering a provocative quote and asking them to consider who might have said it and why is also an appetizer for the main course of class.

As important as it is to capture students' attention and to help them build their attention-focusing skills, it is equally important to recognize when their brains need rest. As noted in the previous chapter, observing students for the signs that precede the glazed expressions of brain burnout and giving a timely syn-*nap* will prevent the state of neurotransmitter depletion.

Students given a short warning before the actual syn-*nap* avoid the frustration of suddenly having to stop an engaging activity before they reach some closure. It also helps students to know if and when they will be coming back to the activity, so they can plan their time accordingly.

Once students' attention focuses, they are empowered to become engaged in their learning process. Using surprise, novelty, and variation to capture and hold their attention activates the centers of the brain needed to begin the process. They will now be ready to use executive functions and higher-order thinking to sift through information, form connections and relationships, and achieve the ultimate goal of placing new knowledge into their memory storage centers. Surprise students today, and you will be rewarded by their successful memory retrieval months from now.

Teachable Moments

Most students have active imaginations and a willingness to open their minds. You have probably observed their passionate reactions to unexpected or unplanned events that ignite their emotions. These moments may occur after an assembly with an inspirational speaker or following a momentous news event, such as the reporting of a devastating tsunami or the death of a prominent politician or celebrity. The teachable moment might come with the announcement that a class member has been diagnosed with cancer, or after a bird flies in through the classroom window. Some teachers try to limit the impact of what they consider distractions. Wise teachers take advantage of the fact that these teachable moments or events already have students at a heightened state of attention and awareness.

These moments do not have to be perceived as a setback to a structured lesson plan, but can be seen as an opportunity to channel the students' emotional stimulation into a focused, powerful brain state of heightened awareness. One strategy for sustaining their connection in the moment is by personalizing the experience with student-centered questions. Follow-up can be about what interested them or frightened them, what they were reminded of, or what touched them. You can also ask them what more they want to know or what they would like to do about what they just saw, experienced, or heard.

Inspirational speakers have primed my students' sensory and emotional brain centers with compelling personal stories about living with physical challenges or years of captivity in a POW camp. After these experiences, we returned to the classroom and kept that sense of being in the moment. The ensuing discussions led to some of the students' highest levels of intellectual processing.

When a wild bird came in a window and flew around in a panic, bumping into walls until he made his ultimate escape through the door we opened, it became an opportunity to open our minds to the teachable moment. The students connected flashbulb and emotional memories into authentic learning about the rights and responsibilities of humans who construct buildings in locations that were former habitats of animals.

Rather than viewing a spontaneous teachable moment as a distraction, planning for these moments in advance facilitates making the most of a moment when one arises unexpectedly. Try taking advantage of the moment to engage students who are already at a heightened state of attention and awareness. To help the teachable moment become a focus rather than a distraction, consider these options to sustain the students' engagement:

• Students write a quickwrite about how the experience made them feel. To do a quickwrite, students write for three to five minutes (depending on age) without ever taking their pencils off the paper. If they don't know what to write, they write the last word again and again until inspiration hits. When time is up, they can silently read what they wrote and underline one or two phrases they consider important. These can be shared with the class, can serve as a prompt for a subsequent, more formal essay about the subject, or can be compiled into a class compendium to be posted on the bulletin board or sent home to parents, a local or school newspaper, or a speaker who motivated them.

• Teachable moments that are more personal, such as seeing a classmate have a seizure, still lend themselves to a quickwrite, after a discussion and explanation including correction of any misconceptions they may have.

• If a student hurts a classmate's feelings, a teachable moment may be valuable if and when the offended student is comfortable with that idea. For example, if one child calls another a "cretin," a class meeting about feelings (not accusations) could be followed by a more scientific session about where words now considered insults came from. (*Cretinism* is the scientific term for the mental retardation associated with low thyroid function, which was sometimes the result of low iodine in the diet.) Showing students the literal meaning of words that have become hurtful names will inform them and take the toxic power away from the word. This approach is a gentle way of reminding students that how they use words is a reflection on their own intelligence.

• Anticipate potential conflicts and consider how to use them as opportunities to create teachable moments. At Williams College, the U.S. presidential election could have been a polarizing event among students. The result could have been distraction from classwork. By bringing a series of politicians and political analysts on campus for dinners, discussions with students, lectures, and debates, the student body and faculty shared common experiences and were energized and educated, rather than polarized, by the election year political process.

• When teachable moments are associated with highly emotional class responses, the shared compassion can enhance the strength of the class community. A communal emotional experience, where students give and receive comfort and understanding from each other, builds bonds that can be recalled during times of conflict. In such times, students can be prompted to recall the caring feelings they once shared. When a series of arguments about handball court rules at recess seemed to be disrupting class harmony, I said, "Remember how we were able to comfort each other after our hamster died? Can we use those caring feelings now as we work out our handball court problems?"

• Questions students raise about the events that inspired the teachable moment have future value. They are imbued with the high emotional importance of that powerful, shared experience. A list of the questions raised by these moments can be collected on a wall chart for future consideration. If the emotional moment was a terrorist act, for example, students may raise questions both philosophical and historical that could be applicable to future history, literature, or even science lessons: Should terrorists who are arrested receive the same rights as other people accused of crimes? Was terrorism ever part of the American struggles for independence or minority rights? How are buildings designed so they fall inwards (implode) instead of exploding outward when powerful detonations occur?

During future lessons about related topics, referring to the questions on the list that the class created during the teachable moment can enhance the personal significance (relational memory) of the lesson. The question, originally written in response to the emotional surge of the attention-grabbing event, will rekindle some of that emotional energy during this new lesson. The students will respond with the heightened engagement and personal connections that make lessons more memorable.

Powerful opportunities arise when students' responses to the emotional impact of teachable moments are supported. These opportunities can help them develop their skills of critical thinking and open-mindedness. After all, aren't those the skills we hope they will call upon in response to emotionally charged issues when they are adults and future leaders? Imagine a citizenry where open-minded analysis and thoughtful judgment prevail during tumultuous times.

Technology to Focus Attention in Class

During a teaching job interview in 1999, I was asked to describe how I would use technology in an ideal classroom. I asked if *ideal* could be taken literally, or if I had to stay within the confines of space, time, and money. Given permission to describe such a classroom without any limitations, I eagerly described my dream of interactive student-teacher communication systems using computer technologies. I'd heard about parts of this techno-classroom being used at the University of California School of Medicine in San Diego and other aspects in place at Vassar College. I added a smattering of my own visions and proceeded to detail the design for teacher-student instant feedback as well as other technology-enhanced, engaging strategies to stimulate focused attention grounded in brain-based learning research. The impressive thing, as I look back upon the classroom I described then, is that advances in technology have made my dream classroom a near reality. I have already instituted some aspects of that hypothetical classroom into my math classes, and I am likely to be teaching with more of them within the next several years.

Initial imaging and brain mapping studies revealed the areas of the brain that are active in attentiveness, specific memory, learning, and information retrieval. Subsequent studies built upon that information to evaluate how these brain-learning centers responded to various teaching strategies and learning environments. The technology is now available to build on professional skills in the art of teaching and through computer programs that captivate focus, assess student interest, and obtain immediate and ongoing feedback about student attention and comprehension while lessons are in progress. Computer technology can help educators design and adjust curriculum and lessons to fit the specific needs of a class in real time. Without waiting for test results at the end of a unit of study, technology can reveal when student attention and comprehension is waning while the lesson is in progress.

Possible Computer Feedback Classroom of the Future

Well-designed programs will be able to provide teacher and student feedback while also individualizing each student's review material to the areas where deficiencies are identified. Technology is also available, albeit only in place in a small number of schools, to give teachers personal and immediate feedback about student comprehension of the lessons they are teaching while they are teaching them. This immediate-feedback screen on the teacher's desktop computer reveals constantly changing data about how attentive the students are, what they already know about the topic, what new material they comprehend as it is explained, and what remains confusing to them after it has been presented. We discern much of this now by watching and listening to students or by questioning them and encouraging them to ask questions during class. Yet we know that some students have learned to appear engaged while daydreaming, and others claim to have no questions even though they don't understand the material.

In the computer-feedback classroom of the not-too-distant future, students will have notebook-sized computers at their desks that directly feed information they input to the teacher's computer screen. (Part of this system is in place in the math classroom at the middle school where I teach, where student calculator data are forwarded to the teacher's computer to compile class data pools in activities such as statistical analysis.)

How Technology Will Help

Two of the greatest impediments to focused attention are lessons that are either not understood to the point of student frustration or are already so well understood that the lesson is not challenging and engaging. Models already exist that give teachers instant feedback if either situation is negatively affecting student attention. Students can push buttons to indicate when they are confused and need more explanation or bored because they already know the material. They can input their individual responses to questions the teacher asks.

Once a teacher asks a question about the material he or she has just gone over, students can each type in their individual yes/no, numerical, or multiple-choice letter answers. Teachers can see a grid showing each student's response and a tabulation about what percentage of the class "gets it" so they can either proceed or teach the material again in another way.

Integrating Interactive Technology

Until interactive classroom technology becomes more readily available, students can turn over color-coded index cards to represent confusion or comprehension at any moment in the lesson, but it won't be long before more interactive technology becomes integrated into the classroom. I can foresee a future where instant feedback in classrooms would be made possible with technology similar to the modules used in audience-participation games and dating shows on TV.

We have all seen the power of computers to engage students' attention through the instant gratification of sight and sound. Sometimes it seems that computers threaten the ability to teach without bells and whistles. A 2005 report by Bonnie Rubin in the *Chicago Tribune* acknowledged, "Kids are multimedia jugglers with bedrooms wired like spaceship cockpits where they do math and English while simultaneously watching TV, surfing the Web, instant messaging, and chatting on cell phones while music pumps out of the ministereo or iPod." Yet this multiple-stimulation environment might not be all bad. Michelle Cottle (2005), writing in the *New Republic*, suggested that "The modern hyperkinetic workplace requires doing what seems like 20 things at every possible moment. So when kids open that algebra book, turn on the TV, fire up the computer, and dial their cell phones, they are not just frittering away the hours. They're preparing for their future careers."

I'm not ready to go that far in supporting computer distractions as a homework accessory to build multitasking skills. However, specific academic computer programs and Web sites can be assets for generating and maintaining students' attention during their practice and review sessions because the technology can arouse their auditory, visual, and kinesthetic sensory brain learning pathways and can make review and practice more enjoyable and efficient than worksheets.

Another way to adjust lessons to the best level of student comfort and challenge is to find out *before* class, and even before a final lesson plan is determined, how much they learned from their reading or homework. Response to reading homework from the previous night can't usually be checked before the day's lesson, but there are other ways to know in advance which aspects of the topic to clarify more carefully and which to cover more quickly. When the course involves a complex textbook in almost any subject, or an AP class when there is not enough class time to review all the information covered in independent reading, students can submit responses to questions posed about the reading they do at home. This is an assignment they must complete before the day of class—actual homework where they e-mail their teacher their brief responses to or brief summaries of the material they read and indicate what parts of the reading confused them. This assignment serves several purposes. It keeps them individually accountable to keep up with the work, they can't forget their homework because they e-mailed it in, and it informs the teacher about the knowledge gaps and strengths.

Teachers read these "response to reading" assignments prior to the next class session and know which parts of the reading the students did understand and therefore don't need further explanation of in class. Reading these responses similarly reveals which parts of the reading were poorly understood and need more clarification during that class period. This feedback process highlights the points to explicitly review in class and avoids the attention-loss pitfalls of lessons that are either not understood to the point of student frustration or are already so well understood that the lesson is not challenging and engaging.

It may seem as if this communication process would extend an already long workday and prep time, but with practice, lessons finetuned to computer-enhanced student feedback become more engaging because they are geared to the students' needs. We know how difficult it is for some students to admit in class that they don't follow the lesson or the text. With this communication system, they feel that their teacher knows what they are confused about and they arrive in class trusting that if they *pay attention,* the questions and responses they e-mailed will be answered without their having to raise their hands.

Systems like these let teachers use technology to bring them closer to their students. The computers serve to unite, not divide. In the previous chapter, the role of technology in memory, especially with regard to reinforcement and rehearsal, was discussed. Now, with the technology at hand or soon to be, educators and curriculum designers can captivate students through manipulation of sight and sound to stimulate their senses and to provide the feedback teachers need to keep student attention high.

Elevating Attention Skills from Casual Awareness to Insightful Observations

You have probably heard about an experiential class taught in most police academy and law school classrooms early in the first weeks of the program. It usually involves a confederate of the teacher who runs into the class, steals the teacher's briefcase, and runs out. The students are then asked to write down all the details they can recall about the description of the intruder and his or her actions. After they have written their "reports," they are told that it was a set-up, and the scene is re-enacted. Predictably, they are astonished and embarrassed at how inaccurate their own "eyewitness" accounts are and they learn the lesson that paying careful and studied attention is quite different from passively watching and hearing something. This observation experience motivates them to work at honing their skills of insightful, active observation, especially in emotionally charged situations when clear thinking is most challenged.

Classroom detectives. The same type of experiences can be used to develop the focused attention skills that students need to develop in school and when doing independent homework. Experiential activities similar to the one used in law enforcement instruction help students practice their attention skills. A confederate not known to the students enters the classroom in the middle of a lesson, does something unusual, and departs.

Students are asked to be eyewitnesses and write down (or very young children can orally report) everything they recall about the surprise visitor and his or her actions. The first time they give their eyewitness accounts, it is without any specific prompts. When they think they have no more observations to report, directed questions are sure to elicit more information. At first, these questions should be concrete, such as: Was he wearing glasses? Did she have straight or curly hair? As the students realize that with prompts they recall more details, they learn the technique of self-questioning.

Practiced observation builds attention skills. After the classroom intruder response about concrete observations, students are asked for more abstract conjectures about why the person came to their classroom. Was he a stranger, or did he seem to know his way around? Did he seem threatening? Where do they think he went upon leaving? With each response, students must give reasons for their interpretations. They are told that professional detectives or investigators in science, medicine, crime labs, and archeology must develop their observation and focused-attention skills to obtain as much information as possible from the objects of their investigations.

After several more similar observation practices, other types of training situations are introduced, such as showing an overhead projection of a scene, reading a passage from a book, or showing a short film. Then students repeat the process of first writing what they recall unprompted, then adding to their observations in response to questions, and finally making interpretations that they must support with evidence. Through repeated practice, they will incorporate the observation-prompting questions they have been repeatedly asked into their own internal observation checklists, thereby increasing the quality and quantity of sensory input they are capable of perceiving accurately.

 Gray Matter

As students practice making interpretations and supporting them, they will be using the abstracting, patterning, ordering, prioritizing, judging, and connecting skills of their frontal lobe executive functions. In terms of brain function and structure, they are starting at a stage of superficial attention where they notice, but don't really *see,* and the information doesn't take root in the memory. As they develop their skills of observing, discriminating patterns and details, and making connections, they are at a higher cognitive level, which stimulates and interconnects more of the brain's memory circuitry. Eventually, new dendrite sprouts will grow and root the new information into the long-term memory storage banks. You will have provided the nourishing dendrite sprout food in the form of the rich sensory environment and experiential learning situations, and their self-confidence as observers who can skillfully direct their attention to take in their world will flourish.

There are significant benefits to professional educators who create exciting, engaging classrooms and curriculum where students' attention is focused. The results will more than offset the additional planning and prep work involved. Smiles will replace groans, eye-rolls, and disruptive behavior; students will be more cooperative and responsive; and even the e-mail and phone calls from parents will become more positive and grateful.

3

HOW STRESS AND EMOTION AFFECT LEARNING

Children remind you of the comfort of simplicity. They have compelling common sense, accessibility, honesty, and lack of pretense.
~ Elizabeth Berg

Peter was an extremely bright, dedicated student with the intellectual potential and constructive ambition to be a high academic achiever. He had moved to the United States from Southeast Asia in 4th grade, and stress from family problems was a powerful emotional burden. In his case, I knew that giving him opportunities for academic challenge and success would let him spend time in his comfort zone: intellectual pursuits. Knowing his situation helped me monitor his stress level and adjust the academic stretches accordingly. Not only did he find the school days a time of respite from the stress at home, but because both he and his wonderful mother put a great deal of value on school success, his excellent and accelerated schoolwork was a source of joy for both of them during their trying times.

> Dear Dr. Willis,
>
> Peter is so proud of you and talks about you all the time to other people. Thank you very much for being the teacher who made the difference. I respect you with all my heart. You have been so kind to us, especially during this hardest time in our lives: separation, divorce, family illness, and death.
>
> The following is what Peter said about you as his 5th grade teacher. "I think that the vocabulary and spelling tests really improved my English. I like the way Dr. Willis teaches. I also like the way she writes

and gives me detailed comments, so that I can correct myself and enhance my writing and reading skills. The way she helped me in the social studies was by teaching me how to take notes and I learned to read the pages and summarize them in notes. These helped me to understand American history.

She is very benevolent. I will miss her very much, but I will also remember how kind she was to me. Among all of my teachers, she is the most knowledgeable teacher for me so far. That's why I respect her very much. Her personality traits made me feel comfortable and respectable. She is the best!"

Sincerely,
(Peter's mom)

We live in a stressful world in troubled times, and that is not supposed to be the way children grow up. School classrooms can be the safe haven where academic practices and classroom strategies can provide children with emotional comfort and pleasure as well as knowledge. When teachers use strategies to reduce stress and build a positive emotional environment, students gain emotional resilience and learn more efficiently and at higher levels of cognition.

Where Did the Joy of Learning Go?

We know that for most children, kindergarten is something anticipated with awe and enthusiasm—especially when one or more older siblings are already in school. Young children may certainly be anxious about starting school, but those anxieties usually revolve around fear of leaving a parent or the security of the home environment. The idea of being a student is exciting. Most kindergarten or 1st grade students speak passionately about what they learn and do in school. Fortunately, there is no condemnation from the usual legislative critics that if these youngest children have fun in school, they are not learning.

In the current state of legislated standardized tests linked to the financial stability of schools, two factors encroach upon the joyous learners by the time they reach 2nd or 3rd grade. There is the pressure for the type of academic achievement that can be measured on standardized tests of superficial rote memory. In addition, many teachers are mistrustful and anxious about how they will be judged by mandated curriculum enforcers or legislative analysts who judge teachers and teaching without the benefit of having been trained as professional educators. Uninformed critics may make the erroneous assumption that if children are laughing, interacting in groups, or being creative with art, music, and dance, they are not doing *real* or important academic work. The result is that teachers have been mandated or feel pressured to preside over more sedate, solemn classrooms with students on the same page in the same book, sitting in straight rows, looking straight ahead at the teacher. These quiet classrooms give the judges who pass by a false sense of security if they think that discipline and order mean *real* learning is taking place.

The truth is that when the joy and comfort are scrubbed from the classroom and replaced with homogeneity, and when spontaneity is replaced with conformity, students' brains are distanced from effective information processing and long-term memory storage.

As has been revealed through neuroimaging studies of the amygdala, the hippocampus, and the rest of the limbic system and through measurement of dopamine and other brain chemical transmitters, students' comfort level has a critical impact on information transmission and storage in the brain. The factors that have been found to affect this comfort level—such as self-confidence, trust and positive feelings for teachers, and supportive classroom and school communities—are directly related to the state of mind that is compatible with the most successful learning, remembering, and higher-order thinking. The highest-level executive thinking, making of connections, and "aha" moments are more likely to occur in an atmosphere of "exuberant discovery," where students of all ages retain that kindergarten enthusiasm of embracing each day with the joy of learning (Kohn, 2004).

Amygdala and Stress

Cutting-edge neuroimaging research described in the earlier chapters referred to PET scans and fMRI scans that reveal significant disturbances in the brain's learning circuits and chemical messengers when subjects are studied in stressful learning environments. In particular, the amygdala becomes overstimulated by stress, and in that hypermetabolic state, information cannot pass from sensory awareness into the memory connection and storage regions of the brain. That is what has been seen when brain activity during learning is visualized on these scans.

No objective neuroimaging or brain wave analysis data demonstrate any negative effects of joy and exuberance in classrooms, yet that has become the spoken or unspoken mandate. Now there is the hard science that proves the negative brain impact of stress and anxiety and the beneficial changes in the brain that are seen when children are motivated by and personally connected to their lessons. It is valuable to students for teachers to become familiar with this evidence and pass it along to parents, administrators, and legislators to promote change from without, but it is critical to begin (or continue) using the strategies that are shown to reduce stress in classrooms. Even before the mandates catch up with the brain research, teachers are the frontline professionals who can use the techniques to keep this generation of students from falling into the abyss of joyless, factory-style education.

When children experience instruction that is founded on brain-based strategies that engage their interests and also reduce stress, they become more successful and happier learners. The common theme to the brain research about stress and knowledge acquisition is that superior learning takes place when stress is lowered and learning experiences are relevant to students' lives, interests, and experiences. Lessons must be stimulating and challenging, without being intimidating, for the increasing curriculum standards to be achieved. Otherwise the stress, anxiety, boredom, and alienation that students experience block the neuronal transmission, synaptic connections, and dendrite growth that are the physical and now visible manifestations of learning.

 Gray Matter

Stress in the classroom or elsewhere, especially when associated with anxiety or fear, releases a chemical called TMT, or trimethyltin, into the brain. TMT disrupts brain cell development. When it is present in brain regions during short stressful periods, there is impaired short-term memory and work efficiency. After extended periods of stress, TMT is associated with reduction in long-term memory storage and retrieval, motivation, and creative problem solving. While students under stress may appear to work "harder," the quality of the work decreases (Kato & McEwen, 2003).

In the hippocampus region, through which data must pass to be encoded as memory, stress-related release of TMT—both acute and chronic—suppresses the growth of dendrites and maintenance of neuron health (McEwen, 1999).

Affective Filter

In 1988, Steven Krashen developed a theory of language acquisition and development that included the hypothesis of an *affective filter.* He described the higher success rate of second language acquisition in learners with low stress and the slower language acquisition for learners when stress was high. He postulated that anxiety and low self-image created a mental blockade that filtered or blocked out new learning (O'Grady, Dobrovolsky, & Aronoff, 1997). Ten years later, a physical structure in the brain that was the manifestation of the affective filter was demonstrated on fMRI scans of the amygdala.

Teachers recognize that a state of anxiety occurs when students feel alienated from their academic experiences or anxious about their lack of understanding. This stressed state happens when a lesson is tedious, not relevant to their lives, confusing, or anxiety-provoking (such as when they don't know the meaning of the vocabulary words in a story or if a math lesson is too fast for them to follow or too slow to hold their interest).

In this stressed state, the information doesn't pass through the amygdala to the higher thinking and memory centers of the brain. If the state of anxiety and stress is prolonged, it can lead to destruction and loss of critical connecting dendrites and synapses in the hippocampus. This means that new information does not reach the brain regions where it needs to be processed, associated with previous knowledge and experience, and stored for later recall.

Clues that student anxiety and stress are excessive.

• What appears to be boredom or acting out may be a response to the stress of confusion.

• When the number of students actively participating in a discussion or offering answers to questions is lower than usual, the material may be at stress level.

• Shortened attention spans are the brain's way of shutting out anxiety-producing confusion about material that is not being presented in an engaging and comprehensible manner.

• Although questions usually indicate some confusion or students' desire for additional information, a sudden drop in the usual number of questions during a difficult lesson may mean confusion and anxiety rather than comprehension. That should be a tip-off that student understanding should be assessed at that point in the lesson.

If it becomes clear that students are struggling to keep up, stop the lesson and ask students to write a few sentences about what they think was the main point of the lesson. After sharing their notes with a partner or two, they may have their confusion resolved, or they may realize that they are not the only ones confused and be more comfortable asking questions. The students who do have clear understanding will know they understand because partners will appreciate their summaries. Those students can be asked to read what they have for the benefit of the rest of the class.

Interventions When Stress Has Become Too High

Given the fact that neuroimaging and qEEG studies of the human brain allow us to see what happens when students are stressed or affected by positive and negative emotions, how can teachers create the environments where destructive anxiety is low while providing enough challenge for suitable brain stimulation for each student?

Purposefully planning for the ideal emotional atmosphere. From brain scan research, we know that pleasurably challenging lessons cause the amygdala to have moderately stimulated metabolism and that this warmed-up state of alert stimulation facilitates the brain's processing of information.

When students are experiencing a lot of stress, often from a lesson that is overly abstract or not understood by students as relevant to their lives, teachers need to find ways to make the lesson more personally interesting, relevant, and motivating. Teaching complex, abstract concepts is an area where it is more critical than ever for teachers to find ways to connect information considered important, or required by standards, to students lives and interests. Unfortunately, textbooks that were going in that direction in the last few decades are having to drop some pages of the "human interest" and personal connections to make room for standardized test practice questions and rote material. One source of this background and connecting material is in the textbooks that were published in the 1990s. Another source of connection is the Internet, where lesson plan–sharing Web sites and even state Web sites for standards provide sources for student activities and information databases that bring the more fact-heavy, cold data lessons to life.

The same measures adults use to reduce stress (enjoying hobbies, time with friends, exercise, music, or socializing) can also reduce student stress. Even though schools are shortening recess, physical education, art, drama, and even lunch hours to add more time for academic lectures, teachers can give students a three-minute vacation to reduce stress. Any pleasurable activity used even as a brief break can give the amygdala a chance to "cool down" and the neurotransmitters time to rebuild as the students are refreshed by joining in a song or listening to the reading of a book they enjoy.

It is always good planning to help students see the relevance or future importance of any lesson. In the ideal situation, at any point in a lesson an appropriate adult should be able to walk into the classroom and have students give reasonable responses to the question, "Why are you learning about this?" It is not always possible to explain the immediate relevance of every lesson, such as in math, where some skills must be mastered before students can go on to the relevant investigation of larger topics. One way to increase relevance is by taking word problems from the text and changing the names to those of students or teachers from the school, or popular celebrities or sports heroes. Similarly, when the problem is about interest rates, have the item being purchased something the students would want to buy such as an iPod or new sneakers. Batting averages are calculated to the thousandth, so that helps increase relevance and therefore student interest about decimal place values.

Ask students themselves to help find relevance. Students appreciate empathy, so it may help to ask, "I know this seems pretty dry and not really important to your own life, but can you think of any way it could sometime be useful?" When a lesson or series of lessons will be heavy on rather dry facts that must be memorized, the stress can be reduced when students see an authentic reward for their mental efforts, such as the opportunity to participate in a stimulating hands-on discovery laboratory exploration once they master the information they need for background. Then not only will they have a better emotional attitude about what they are learning, but the information will have more relational connections to hold it in long-term memory storage.

More strategies for low-stress classrooms. Eliminating all stress from students' lives is impossible. However, even if previous classroom experiences have led to associations and memories that link certain activities, such as multiplication tables, to a stress response from the amygdala, students can be helped by the chance to revisit the activity in a positive setting. You can make the activity less stressful by not calling on students in front of their classmates and not making the learning process a competition honoring only the student who answers a multiplication flash card first. Then positive associations can be connected to multiplication when the student practices with a positively reinforcing strategy. This process could be first reviewing the table for multiplying by eight, followed by filling in blanks on a worksheet and immediately checking each written answer with a calculator. There is instant positive reinforcement if the answer is correct. Even if it is incorrect, there is inherent pleasure in seeing the calculator produce the right answer—much more so than hearing a classmate call out the answer before the challenged student can even begin to think of it.

In a similar way, students can build upon their neurochemical reserves of positive feelings by taking the time to savor successes and being reminded of them. This reinforcement can be accomplished when their names are posted on the "success" list. Rather than a competitive list of math table scores, teachers can put up names of students who achieve personal goals (such as multiplying by eights), recognizing them for "Personal Goal Achievement."

Another way to decrease stress is to help students prioritize the important information. This prioritizing is especially critical in later school years, when the textbooks are longer and independent reading is required. Even in elementary school, students benefit from learning how to cull important information from each paragraph in a social studies book or science book. Prioritizing can be part of note-taking instruction or discussed verbally. When teachers demonstrate and explain how they prioritize, it gives students instruction in how to make those judgments for themselves as they read texts and study for exams independently. Reducing the amount of information a student needs to deal with is a valuable stressbuster.

Finally, remember that interest and discovery drive achievement, and students are more likely to remember and really understand what they learn if they find it compelling or have some part in figuring it out or discovering it for themselves. In addition, when interest in high, stress and anxiety are decreased and students are more accepting of their errors, more willing to try again, and less self-conscious about asking questions. Because of their increased focus, they are more likely to comprehend information that might otherwise be challenging for them.

Predictability Can Reduce Anxiety and Increase Creativity

Until this point, most of the stress and anxiety discussed has related to confusion prompted by overly challenging material, boredom from lessons of subject matter already mastered or without personal relevance, or the stress of students sitting in overly structured classes following mandated, inflexible curriculum.

The letter at the beginning of this chapter touched on the issues of the high-stress world our students live in globally and in the microcosms of their community or families. When research-based strategies are used to make the classroom community a safe, nurturing environment, that will help lower the stressed state of students' affective filters (amygdala and hippocampus) when they enter the classroom.

Before students can focus on academics, they must feel physically safe and emotionally secure. A 2004 Independent School Management study surveyed parents as to the main reason they sent their children to private schools. The number one reason was safety—both physical and psychological. One of the determinants of what made a school psychologically safe was predictability, because predictability lowers stress and increases confidence. In those schools that rated high in predictability, students and parents understood what actions resulted in what responses. There was a confidence that teachers would be predictable and consistent in their behavior and expectations, so students could predict the outcome of their actions. That consistency reduced stress. Students should be challenged in the classroom, but they need to feel certain about their teachers' expectations, grading systems, fairness, availability, and responsiveness. If students are confident about predictability in those areas, they can feel supported to explore and take creative risks.

One way to build this community is by incorporating specific stress-reducing and community-building strategy instruction into classroom learning. When a teachable moment comes up in class or in a book the class is reading, that can be an opportunity to explicitly teach students about reducing stress, controlling impulses, delaying gratification, expressing feelings, or being a proactive friend.

Teachers can be the infrastructure of a strong community where students feel safe, supported, and trusted enough to channel their enthusiasm into explorations. This freedom to explore allows students to return to the mind-set they had when they started kindergarten and felt free to believe that every career was within their reach. When teachers take the time to make connections with their students, they become the positive, and sometimes only, consistent influence in students' tumultuous lives. Especially during adolescence, the power of a teacher to make a permanent difference in a student's life and potential is incalculable.

When Some Stress Can Be a Good Thing

First came the neuroimaging confirmation that high stress causes overload, with excessive metabolism in the amygdala blocking the passage of information into the rest of the brain. Subsequent studies demonstrated that when the amygdala is *mildly* stimulated there can be enhanced information transit through the brain.

As noted previously, when the metabolic activation in the amygdala is mild to moderate, and not excessive, new sensory input (learning information) passes more quickly through the limbic system into the brain centers of higher cognition, executive function, and memory storage. An environment perceived as frightening and overwhelming slows the learning process down, but a little excitement and encouragement can help build enthusiasm.

As the sensory data pass through the "preheated" (but not overloaded) amygdala and hippocampus, they are encoded with emotional meaning. Information with positive emotional connection is retained more successfully. That is why the ideal type of instruction is one that is punched up with interesting surprise and positive emotional experiences such as novelty, the social pleasure of group or partner work, or the fun of physical movement, art, music, quiz-show format, or computer simulations.

 Gray Matter

There appears to be a link between the release of the hormones cortisone and adrenaline and the response to stress. When the stress is a manageable but stimulating challenge, rather than a threat, these hormones (released in the right quantities) result in memory improvement. It is when the cortisol is released in high amounts over sustained periods of time that it appears to result in shrinkage of the cells in the hippocampus (Kohn, 2004).

In small amounts ACTH, a cortisone-releasing hormone, has a positive alerting effect. It is released in response to pleasant surprise, novelty, and positive personal associations. When these feelings are linked to new learning, the released ACTH promotes growth of new dendrites and synaptic connections between neurons. This creates additional circuits and connections between the new information and existing knowledge for greater recall and higher-order thinking (LeDoux, 1997).

During positively emotional states, when neuroimaging shows metabolic mild stimulation in the amygdala, students tested showed better focus, memory enhancement, improved reading and writing, increased decision-making abilities, and the more flexible thinking needed to stimulate creative ideas for problem solving. They even were observed to have social behaviors of greater helpfulness, sociability, and patience.

Teachers have the capacity to fine-tune the level of stimulation versus stress in the classroom to achieve the right balance that inspires positive brain response and avoids the stressors that impair brain efficiency and effective behavior.

Adolescent Stress

Teenage Brain Development

Although teenager's bodies are reaching maturity, their brains are undergoing developmental changes that can cause erratic behavior. The prefrontal cortex is the last part of the brain to mature. This brain region is the center for emotional stability, moral reasoning, judgment, and executive functions such as concentration, planning, delayed gratification, and prioritizing. Because of the fluctuations in the developing prefrontal cortex, teens might have difficulty communicating ideas and feelings, making wise decisions, or establishing consistent self-identities.

This incomplete brain development means that teens will be emotionally labile, unpredictable, and prone to blow out of proportion things that affect their lives. Until this brain maturation is complete and hormonal stasis is achieved, events or changes that seem inconsequential to adults may seem huge to young teens and can provoke stress. An important way to help teens through this period of flux is to provide them with a sense of community and to help them build their stores of self-confidence.

Build Confidence by Building Community and Connectedness

> *Our job is not to be the opposition to their ideas, but to be flexible, living, breathing, organic, changing and responsive to students' ideas to help them embrace their dreams so they can channel their enthusiasm positively rather than cut it off because they don't conform to a lesson plan.*
>
> ~ Eric Lehman

Planning and providing the most effective emotional atmosphere is especially important for teens. At the time when brain development and hormone release are in high gear, school community and teacher connections can support students to help them deal with the years of physiological tumult. The goal is to reduce the stress that impairs effective learning and memory by building student confidence during these teen years of struggle with identity development.

The years of middle school and high school are the time when teens need to develop individualized identities, often through supportive interactions with social peer groups and role model adults. At Santa Barbara Middle School, where I teach, and other schools where student confidence is nurtured during the stressful teenage years, several common factors are evident:

• Teachers take the time to listen to students and acknowledge the value of their opinions and ideas.

• Students trust (through predictability built upon experience) that adults who understand their mood swings and energy surges and dips will support them.

• Teachers embrace students' unique qualities and give them opportunities to be honored for their individuality.

• A school community of respect is modeled, valued, and consistently enforced.

• Thoughtfully structured academic, athletic, physical, and emotional challenges are scaffolded with the preparation and tools needed for all students to succeed at their highest potential.

• Schoolwide acknowledgments of success in town meetings or assemblies honor more than "best" athlete or academic. Recognition is authentic for students reaching their individual goals, helping classmates, and contributing community or school service.

A student's note of gratitude to the faculty and staff, received 20 years after she went on to high school, underscores the benefit of a strong school community:

> Our school gave me a safe place to explore and push myself academically, physically, and socially. The teachers cared and I knew they enjoyed their work. As students, we made real connections with the teachers and saw them as friends as well as mentors. That created an environment that promoted learning beyond the 'norm.'

Faculty collaboration. Faculty meetings can be an opportunity to work together to help individual students going through stressful periods. Prior to a meeting, teachers who are concerned about unusual behavior or academic performance of particular students can circulate the students' names. This advance notice gives colleagues a chance to check their records and recollections for any recent changes they have noted in these students.

At the meeting it may become evident that Rachael is sleepy and does not bring in assignments on Mondays. Further digging reveals that she stays at her father's apartment on weekends, goes to bed late, and doesn't have access to a computer there. If James is particularly irritable and disruptive in all his afternoon classes, it may be that the teacher on lunch recess duty recalls that he has not been playing basketball with the friends he'd been with previously. The computer teacher may realize he's been spending lunch in the computer room alone. Combining the information from his teachers' observations can start the process of discovering how to help him reconnect with the former friends or find new ones. His history teacher can place him in a group of well-suited classmates for potential new friendships when the class is divided into groups for the next cooperative project, or the music teacher can encourage him to join the new synchronized drum club being formed.

Academic relevance. At a time in their lives when students are absorbed with discovering their own values and identities, it requires more powerful tools to show them directly how their academic subjects are relevant to their lives. It might serve in early elementary school to show that fractions are important because they help us divide a pie equally among six friends. It will take more than that to emotionally connect a teen to algebra.

Faculty collaboration can help increase students' emotional-academic connectedness by increasing academic relevance. These connections can be facilitated through the development of cross-curricular integration based on themes of relevance to teens. Subjects such as prejudice, corruption, and personal freedom can be connected to almost all academic subjects and can be tailored to suit curriculum standards.

Corruption can be the lens through which to view the carpet-baggers in the post–Civil War South, the character flaws in Dickens's *Oliver Twist* or *Tale of Two Cities*, the corrupting or corrosive effects of water that rusts metal, the analysis of some critics that modern art was a corruption of standards of beauty, and the misleading statistical analysis of *outliers* (single numbers that fall far from the rest of the numbers in a data pool resulting in misleading mathematical averages).

Self-discovery through academic exploration. As teenagers transition to young adults they struggle to find their personal identities, values, and goals. Teachers can help by providing opportunities for them to build their skills of analysis, critical thinking, and judgment in academic areas. The frontal lobe executive functions that students use to think critically and analytically and to prioritize and organize in their school subjects are the same higher thinking skills that can help them make good decisions when faced with the emotional stressors and ethical dilemmas of their lives outside the classroom.

Teachers can help students develop these executive functions by doing the following:

• Asking open-ended, thought-provoking questions.

• Encouraging students to question what they hear or read in newspapers and to look for author bias in textbooks, thematic meaning in literature, and alternative ways of solving math problems.

• Encouraging students to find their own connections between what they learn in one subject and the course material in their other subjects to develop skills of judgement and critical analysis.

• Teaching students how to evaluate their own learning processes through metacognition to develop the skills that will also help them cope with the challenges they confront daily in this period of life transition.

The more adolescents develop their frontal lobe executive functions, the more engaged they will be in the academic subjects they need to study and the more successfully they will process, remember, and use what they learn.

Personal interest and support. Teachers can increase student connectedness by looking for reasons for student behavior, especially negative changes, rather than simply reacting. When students have been absent, it is the usual response to give them information about the work they missed when they return to class. When teachers go a step further and ask if everything is all right, it establishes a bond with the students. Of course, this approach needs to be done in a non-threatening way and must not appear to be an accusation to see if the absences were justified: "I missed you these past two days. Is there anything I can do to help you get caught up?"

Similarly, if there is an excused absence for a school-approved event such as a special sporting competition or important family event, by making a note in the plan book that the reason for the excused absence was a state soccer tournament, it will be a reminder to ask the student how the games went. Even asking about their out-of-school weekend activities adds to teens' sense of belonging and is one more way to prevent the alienation that is so often part of adolescence.

It is understandable that in large middle and high schools, there needs to be a system of dealing with the chaos of making schedules to suit each student's needs while also considering the availability of teachers and class offerings. Most parents understand rules such as, "There can be no schedule changes during the first week because classes are still in flux and student enrollment is not confirmed until after the first week of school. Please bear with us as we do our best. We will be available to meet with you or your child after that first week when we know the final class offerings and availability."

Fair enough? Yes. The best we can do? Perhaps not. When teachers and counselors consider what students and parents are going through when they are distressed about what seems to be an omission or improper class placement, there is something the counselor or teacher can do to help the year start out with less stress and anxiety. Just a phone call (even though it might add up to 20 phone calls or e-mails) to let the student and family know that their concern is recognized can be the beginning of a relationship of trust and cooperation.

I experienced this support firsthand when my daughter's guidance counselor, Susan Snyder, called me before school started to let me know there was a space in my daughter's schedule that could be a study hall, but because Alani had a strong interest in marine biology, that was also a course option. I've taught at and attended public and private schools, and Ms. Snyder's extra efforts at a public high school with several thousand students speaks to the opportunities that individuals have to bring students and their families into the school community through connectedness and support.

Supporting young teens means acknowledging their special interests or talents, even when they seem to change as often as their hair color. It means not overreacting when teens "go ballistic" for reasons we cannot fathom. With patience, humor, and knowledge about the working of the teenage brain, teachers can be the wind that supports their wings and propels them toward their dreams.

Family connections. During elementary school, parents are included in their children's school life through class parties, productions, or sports or as classroom volunteers and field trip chaperones. In junior and senior high school, teenagers seek more separation from parents and closer bonds with classmates, or just independence in general. Nevertheless, to increase their emotional comfort, it is valuable for them to know that through shared activities and communications there is a support system between parents and the adults in their school lives.

These connections can be achieved by parent-student-teacher conferences, school-community service projects, evening speakers about topics of interest to parents and students (a shuttle astronaut or Olympic athlete), parent-teacher-student trips to a special sports or cultural event, and parent volunteers at school extracurricular activities.

Often teachers appreciate the work of the PTA but don't feel connected to it as participants in a partnership with parents. In some schools it is called the PTSA and includes students. With the structure already in place and willing parents, teachers can be the glue that pulls students, parents, and school together.

Looking at physically mature teens can cause adults to forget that the brain is the last part of the human body to mature fully. While these teens look and sometimes act the part of young adults, their frontal lobe executive functions are still underdeveloped. In fact, judgment is one of the last cerebral functions to complete development. The guidance and structure they receive during these years are critical for their safety and for promoting their future as lifelong learners and active participants in a democratic society.

Physical inclusion. Encouraging participation in physical activities is especially important during the teen years. It not only helps stabilize hormonal swings but also gives students a sense of having some control over their bodies during this time of body image doubts and pressures. For students who are not comfortable with team sports, schools can help by offering exercise, dance, or even brisk walking classes as P.E. options. The latter has the advantage of providing a chance for students to talk with an adult outside the walls of the classroom, making the interpersonal connections more informal and often more authentic and supporting.

Teacher-student hikes, bike rides, or even camping trips can deepen students' comfort and sense of belonging. The combination of being outdoors in a supportive group, doing a nonacademic activity with teachers as companions, not critical judges, can relieve the tensions that build within the classroom walls. Even playing handball or four-square with students at recess (instead of supervising from the side, giving students the message that they are not trustworthy) will increase students' sense of school community and acceptance.

In addition, the physiological effects of physical activity include increased cerebral blood flow and oxygen to the brain, the growth of additional capillaries to keep up with brain growth, and increased release of dopamine and serotonin to help sustain attention and concentration (Geyer, 2004).

Academic performance and behavior improve when stress is reduced and emotional comfort is raised. Consider what other opportunities can be offered to students to help them explore new experiences, develop potential interests and friendships, and feel more connected to school. These opportunities can be through clubs, school or class community service projects, or lunchtime mini-productions or sing-alongs. The ideal is to find activities where the best athlete or most outgoing or talented students are not the featured participants over and over. When the activities ensure inclusion, they help students see identity options, not roadblocks.

The brain-based learning research reinforces the need for classrooms to once again become places where the imagination, spirit, and curiosity of students are encouraged, rather than left outside in the playground when the school bell rings.

4

ASSESSMENT THAT
BUILDS DENDRITES

Imagination is more important than knowledge.

~ Albert Einstein

Einstein's opinion about imagination is a worthy one. Without imagination and investigation of ideas, our collective fund of knowledge would stagnate. We do need assessment to determine what students learn and understand, but we can incorporate imagination in the creation of assessments and ensure that students' imaginations, creative thought, and higher executive functions are incorporated into assessments. In that way, assessments become learning experiences that grow more dendrites!

Well-designed assessments give teachers the information necessary to fairly and accurately evaluate the depth of students' understanding. Traditional and especially standardized tests assess only a few parameters, such as rote memory, ability to follow instructions, organization, and time management. Testing that emphasizes those parameters gives students the message that those are the qualities of thinking that are the most valued.

For dynamic educators who believe in the potential for all students to grow by accumulating not only facts but also wisdom, assessments can go beyond measuring rote memory and time management. Creative problem solving and critical analysis are the goals of high-level instruction. These skills can be given the value they merit by being included in student assessment. This expanded assessment process can be achieved while simultaneously building students' strategies for successful responses on standardized tests.

Instruction based on learning research emphasizes the brain's processing of information by patterning. When teaching style is geared to help students find meaning and patterns in the material they study and the relevance of that information to their lives and world, their brains respond by successful pattern formation and information storage in long-term memory. When information is processed and stored in relational patterns, it is accessible for retrieval from multiple cues. That means that there are multiple ways to access these stored memories and bring them into frontal lobe executive function brain regions when the information can be used (Olsen, 1995).

Changing Skills for a Changing Workforce

With the computer and technological progress of recent decades, there is diminishing need for administrative support employees to type, file, keep books, and sort papers. These jobs are done more and more with paperless computer efficiency. Robotic technology is reducing the need for assembly line workers. With these declines in blue collar and administrative support worker jobs, school instruction and assessment must also change to ensure that graduates will have the knowledge to make them valuable and irreplaceable in the work force.

At a 2005 summit meeting of the nation's governors, Bill Gates called American high schools obsolete for not teaching students what they need to know today. He compared the training tomorrow's work force is getting to trying to teach students about modern computers by having them learn how to operate 50-year-old mainframe computers that need data entry cards and fill half a classroom. In his opinion, the high schools of today were designed 50 years ago to meet the needs of another age, and now need upgrading to keep pace with the work force needs of the 21st century.

With this changing employment picture at hand, it is becoming more important to help students learn and succeed in assessments of skills that computers and robots cannot perform. These abilities have been described as *expert thinking* and *complex communications*.

These skills are essentially components of the executive function higher conceptual thinking that takes place beyond rote learning. Expert thinking involves recognizing and organizing patterns and relationships and identifying and solving new problems as they arise.

Complex communication includes careful listening and observing to elicit, interpret, and convey critical information. An example of skilled communication is the citing of relevant evidence in essays, reports, and spoken responses. Citing evidence is one of the major benchmarks in scoring the SAT Writing Assessment, and students will benefit from practice in that skill as early as possible in their education. Once students receive the teaching they need to acquire this fund of knowledge and skills, their assessments can become learning experiences to hone their complex communication skills.

Standardized testing is currently an unavoidable aspect of assessment. To prepare students for success in the careers where their generation will find opportunities, assessments also need to test and acknowledge the frontal lobe executive functions of expert thinking and complex communication.

Assessment Over Time—From Macro to Micro

Yearlong assessment. Although assessments ideally take place during each class period and lesson, planning the year's major unit assessments while planning curriculum builds authenticity into those assessments. Starting the year with clear communication to students about the goals of their studies and expectations for their assessments sets a pattern that gives them the security that accompanies predictability.

Strategize from the start. Take the following steps to ensure that students are aware of assessment expectations:

1. Gauge the assumptions that students have about what is expected of them and how they will be assessed. This evaluation can be an open-ended discussion including their opinions about the purpose of assessments.

2. Offer students the opportunity to express their expectations of what they would look for in assessing a good teacher. This exercise can produce a rubric of what students expect in a teacher: someone who

is fair, trustworthy, doesn't play favorites, cares about them as individuals, and listens when they have legitimate problems and conflicts. Students are appreciative when they are given a chance to "grade the teacher" on these agreed-upon expectations.

3. Discuss your expectations for your students. (After the discussion about students' expectations for their teacher, they are more receptive to hearing about teacher expectations as to what constitutes a successful student.)

4. Provide samples of student work from past years in a binder, including the rubrics used and the grades received. These samples will give students concrete information about teacher expectations. The samples need to relate to assignments similar in character to theirs, but not be the same specific topics. In that way the students will have the opportunity to emulate quality and creativity, not content.

When teacher expectations are accompanied by sincere acknowledgment that all students will be given the opportunity to be successful, regardless of what test scores and grades are in their records, they will have more self-confidence and less anxiety. If students feel safe and in control of their potential for success, they will experience a reduction in affective filters and a reduction in the test anxiety that may have lowered their test performance in previous years.

Rubrics Involve Students in Assessment

Predictability is a critical element in a positive learning environment. The limbic system and affective filter become most responsive to efficient information processing with the assurance of predictability. In addition, the neuronal circuitry is attuned to patterns, so predictable sequences of behavior and response are brain compatible for processing and remembering.

Rubrics that teachers use to assess student work and progress are powerful tools for predictability and patterning. They provide an outline of the criteria that will be evaluated in determining the final grade. This knowledge allows students to understand the relationship between their work, attitude, and effort and the ultimate measurement of their success and achievement. This connection of effort to success is beneficial to all students, but especially for students with

ADD, associating practice with mastery and success can be a break-through.

Teachers almost always use rubrics to determine grades, even if these are unconscious and intuitive. Before writing a rubric, think about what the goal of the assignment is and what the ideal end product would look like. When the rubric is written down and offered to students at the beginning of a new assignment or unit of study, they become partners with the teacher in the process of achieving success. Students are more engaged and confident because they see a predictable process where the outcome is clearly the result of specifically defined input.

In addition, rubrics offer specific goals in multiple areas of achievement, not just a final product. These usually include effort, organization, prioritizing, judgment, analysis, cooperation, proper use of resources, focus, and metacognition. It is not surprising that these are the same qualities that fall under the umbrella of frontal lobe executive function—the highest forms of true learning and cognition.

Students' responses the first time they are given a rubric and told that it is what the teacher will use to determine their grade are uplifting. They feel as if they have been given the answer key to a test. In a way, that is true. Finally they understand that the outcome of their academic success as measured by a grade is indeed completely within their control. If they are willing to put in the effort, they see the path they need to follow to achieve success.

Visualization aids. Web sites such as RubiStar (http://rubistar. 4teachers.org/) offer online tools that allow educators to create customizable rubrics in English and Spanish. They offer templates and preformed rubrics with gradations in assessment for multiple subjects, categories of analysis, and weighting. When students are given the rubrics at the time of their assignments, they can take advantage of opportunities for visualization of success and for daily or weekly self-assessment.

Earlier, visualization was mentioned as a way of preprogramming the neuronal circuits for activation, the way athletes visualize the movements they want their muscles to make. Visualizing brings the brain circuits online to direct those movements. The rubric serves as a visualization stimulus for the brain circuitry that will be called upon in the learning process. Neuroimaging of brains when students begin to *think* about a specific type of learning show activation in the area of the brain that controls that particular type of learning. For example, the frontal executive function areas become more metabolically active as subjects think of organizational strategies needed to prepare material for a debate, even before they are given the debate topic.

Rubrics help students know what to strive for to obtain good grades or produce exemplary projects. They also help students get started and understand the big picture of the assignment. Students experience less stress because what might be perceived as a massive project is broken down into sections.

Rubrics match with executive functions. The prefrontal cortex executive function of planning involves maintaining one main goal while working on subgoals for achieving that goal. Rubrics are like blueprints to guide executive function so students can plan, select from alternatives (prioritize), and monitor and adjust their focus to suppress distracting material and keep on task (Koechlin et al., 1999).

Rubrics correlate effort with success. Using rubrics to help students correlate their effort to their success is a valuable tool. This process works best when students receive feedback at least weekly on a project or in a subject area. They first complete their effort rubric with a self-rating of 1 to 4 in the preset categories. For example, under the category of focus there could be four gradations from which they select the one that best fits their behavior:

1. I worked with focus to complete the task, and when I didn't know the answer right away I tried to work it out or look it up before asking for help.

2. I worked with focus to complete the task, but I asked for help as soon as I didn't know the answer right away.

3. I worked with focus most of the time, but I gave up when I didn't know the answer.

4. I did very little focused work.

(An alternative to the 1 to 4 ranking is the use of descriptive words—e.g., Excellent, Good, Needs Improvement—followed by the worded description of that rating.)

After students complete their rubrics, there is a place for peer or teacher assessment on the week's work. By maintaining these effort-achievement charts for several weeks or the length of the project, students will see how their effort and achievement correlate. The power of that visual proof correlating effort to achievement provides the most predictable and dependable tool that students can have to drive their self-actualization as learners. With a visual model, they see that their level of success is completely in their control, because honest assessment of effort will correspond to their achievement ratings.

An additional benefit to rubric-assisted assessment is in the area of complex communication skills (such as those required in their future workplace or the writing portion of the SAT). The rubric used by the SAT essay graders is also available to students and teachers. When students are experienced in working with rubrics to self-evaluate the quality of the separate aspects of their work, they are prepared to respond to the writing SAT. They are also better prepared for future assignments, even from teachers who don't provide rubrics, as they develop the capacity to develop rubrics and schedules on their own.

What to include in rubrics. In addition to the traditional areas of assessment such as following instructions, citing examples/giving evidence, neatness/organization, and completeness, consider the message students get when certain topics are included in rubrics. As mentioned at the beginning of the chapter, expert thinking and complex communications are important skills for this generation of students. Including these as rubric categories emphasizes such components as recognizing and organizing patterns and relationships, identifying and solving problems, and listening carefully and communicating clearly with others.

The more specific the rubric is in terms of expectations, the more likely the students will feel capable of achieving success. Instead of saying that a top score of 4 in completeness means that "All questions will be answered in detail," a more specific rubric could state, "All questions will be clearly incorporated into the report by using topic sentences that tell the reader what information will follow that answers the question. Excellent responses to questions will include three cited sources of evidence and one personal opinion about the question."

To emphasize the behaviors that promote positive classroom and school communities and create the positive brain states that accompany social stability, rubric categories can recognize attitude, effort, and what students have done to reach the study habit goals set during their last student-teacher conference.

Just as graphic organizers can be more effective when they are student-designed, students benefit from participating in the construction of their rubrics. Involving students in this assessment aspect of their work helps engage them in their learning. With more personal connection, more of their brains are activated. Especially for group work, students can create rubrics with which they will rate their own effort, contributions, and cooperation as well as those of their partners.

Quickwrite Rubric Alternatives

Not every activity or lesson lends itself to the creation of a formal rubric. For these lessons, students can create personal goals in a few sentences. For example, if the lesson involves taking notes during the viewing of a video about the Fertile Crescent in Mesopotamia, students can be told why the video was selected and why the teacher thinks it is important. Students can then think for one minute and write for two minutes about why they think it would be valuable for their notes to be complete and what they will do to achieve that goal.

> I want to know why this part of history is important to my life and my future. I have learned this year that some of the things I study about history help me understand why things happen today. I believe people can learn from mistakes and from successes. I also know that when I took good notes and read them before the last test it helped me more than just reading the book. Last month some of my notes were messy and I couldn't read them. This time I will write my words larger so even if I rush I will still be able to figure out what I meant when I read them later.

If time allows, sharing these goals with partners will deepen the students' commitment to what they wrote and allow students to share ideas. Because the students created their own goals, they will have the personal connection that increases focus and builds stronger cortical relational memory circuits.

When the lesson or unit is over, or at intervals during a longer unit, students benefit when they reread their goals and reflect on their achievement. Asking students to share with the class their successful progress toward goal achievement will build their dopamine-reward system to further strengthen positive behavior and executive function.

A final prompt to stimulate metacognition would be to ask students to think-pair-share or write what they learned about the successful strategies that worked for them to achieve their goals and what obstacles came up that they would want to avoid in the future.

Ongoing Assessment and the Blind Spots

One of the most successful strategies for engaging students' brains in their lessons comes from personal connection and accountability. When students are in a class where teachers ask questions using alphabetical order of students' names or according to seating, students often tune out until their turns, and again after their turns. This predictable routine leads to lowered alertness and brain wave patterns that may resemble drowsiness. Behavior management problems arise when students are not personally connected to these predictable response formats. Generally, if they know that only one right answer is expected or that once they answer a question in sequence they are not going to be directly included in the dialogue for some time, their alerting mechanisms wind down, and information is no longer expedited into memory.

In most subjects and classes, we tend to teach for a week or two and test on that material only after the extended period of the unit of study. A more brain-attuned method is to assess daily and even several times during a lesson to see what students understand. That is neuro-*logical*, because if knowledge gaps are not corrected early, the brain will fill in blanks with misinformation. This misinformation may be stored as long-term memories that are difficult to change once embedded.

An example of the brain filling in information gaps is the eye's physiological blind spot. Visual information is carried to the occipital lobe of the brain after first entering the optic nerve in the back of the eye. The retina (along the back wall of the eye where the rods and cones receive visual data) is disrupted for the several millimeters where the optic nerve pokes through the back of the eye. That means that slightly to the right of the central vision of each eye there is a "blind spot" where no light or image is perceived by the retina. Where the circle of the optic nerve sits there can be no retinal rods and cones to respond to pick up visual data. We don't notice those circular gaps in our vision because the brain fills in the blank spaces with what it predicts would be there based on the pattern of the surrounding visual input.

In the case of information the brain creates to complete patterns, there is the chance it will be incorrect, and only frequent assessment will pick up these errors in working memory before they become stored as long-term memory.

Daily Individual Mini-Assessments

Ongoing assessments and accountability are important for knowing how student comprehension really matches teacher expectations. Experienced teachers usually have some idea what their students' grade ranges (and more importantly, their subject comprehension) are after the first several weeks of school. This is not because they frequently check their grade books, but because they assess student understanding during each lesson—sometimes more than once.

There is a fine line between avoiding the stress of calling on students when they are confused or uncomfortable speaking in front of the whole class and the need to frequently assess each student's engagement and comprehension. There is also the need for students to feel comfortable asking for clarification so misinformation does not become stored in long-term memory.

Children who have lower academic expectations for themselves tend to ask for help less often. Teachers who emphasize self-improvement and effort and who encourage creative problem solving and risk taking, rather than competitive comparisons of student ability, encourage students to ask for help. When students focus on how well they personally have improved rather than on comparing themselves to others, they will be more comfortable asking for help (Ryan, 1998).

Embedding ongoing assessment into everyday curriculum can be done by incorporating performance tasks into learning activities. Ways to keep students engaged, incorporate learning activities into assessments, and ensure correct understanding while doing ongoing assessment include the following:

• Students are given cards with questions when they enter the classroom. The answers to their cards' questions are posted on answer cards that label the seats or tables where they will sit that day. For example, the card might say, "What state is across the northern border of Oregon?" The student will search for the seat or table labeled "Washington."

• Students simultaneously, at the count of three, hold up the colored or white side of an index card when the class is asked a yes/no or true/false question to signal their opinions.

• Students have whiteboards, erasable markers, and cloths (the use of whiteboards is often a treat for students). They write answers in a few large words or numbers in response to questions and hold them up simultaneously after the teacher gives adequate time for all to write an answer. This student response process gives instant teacher feedback as to who needs further explanation.

• For students too reluctant to ask questions that the whole class hears, a colored card can be taped by one end to their desks. Students can flip the card from its white side to its red side if they want the teacher to come by and answer a question privately. In a computer lab, a cup taped to the top side of the computer can be flipped up so that it rests on top of the monitor, signaling the need for help.

• When students are working independently or in small groups, teachers can move around the classroom listening to student discussions and can discover what part of the material needs further explanation.

• Rather than storing incorrect information, students can stop their work periodically and check answers that are posted (after first displaying their work to a teacher to see that they did the work). If they know that they will be credited for corrected errors as well as for trying the work, they can mark their errors in a different color and later show that they made corrections in a different color.

• Multiple answers: This assessment may take the form of asking several students for their answer to the same question even if the first student's answer was correct. Similarly, once an answer is given, students can raise hands if they agree or disagree.

This response process can be used for questions where more than one supported opinion can be a valid response—when backed up by reasons. It also works for pragmatic subjects such as determining the height of a building using a measurement of its shadow. In the mathematical example, although there is a single correct answer, the concept of ratio and proportion and how to use these concepts to solve the problem can be understood and described in multiple ways. This may seem like a process that takes away from valuable teacher instruction, but it actually benefits all students and the teacher. For the teacher, ongoing assessment is taking place so adjustments can be made to alter instruction for the confused students. For students listening who already have an understanding of the concept, it is valuable for them to alter their perspective to understand the alternate approach used by a classmate. For the students who did not understand the concept from the teacher or text explanation, their classmate's approach might be the one that makes sense to them.

Homework Accountability

When students start homework in class (where they are prompted to carefully read instructions and ask questions if they come up) they are more likely to be confident that they can continue successfully at home. It is surprising how many students think of homework as something they need to do for their grades, rather than something they will learn from.

To bring accountability and individual assessment to math homework, my students start math homework in class, and I have the answers available for them to self-correct. They know that they will get full credit for homework if they clearly mark their errors and then show the work they did to get to the correct answer. This immediate feedback of allowing them to check their own work keeps students from repeating the same errors and reinforcing them in their memory.

Students are accountable for learning from their homework. All math homework assignments are shown to me during class time (when students are working on homework or independent or group math projects). When they turn in their self-corrected homework, I give them a paper with a single problem on it. I have an assortment of these so students don't receive the same ones as their neighbors. They must sit at the desk next to mine and solve a problem that is just like those on the homework they just turned in. Accountability is immediate because students do not get homework credit if they cannot solve the new homework problem. If their error is related to simple arithmetic and not to the concept, they are given a second chance.

If their error is related to incomplete understanding of the concept, they meet with me and the other students who need reteaching. After that, they are required to do another similar homework assignment on the same material, but this time they may not work with a partner. When they realize that they don't get credit if they don't learn the material, a shift in their concept of the value of homework takes place. They realize that working with a friend or parents to just get the correct answer will not be adequate for them to learn the concept. They see that homework has a real purpose.

Dendrite Food

Just as the process of summarizing is a valuable memory booster, it is also a way to assess the day's learning. This summarizing is dendrite food, because it makes new learning connections that can grow into more dendrites.

Students write down what they think was the main point or concept of the lesson on note cards. The next day, the best note cards are returned to the students who wrote them and they read them aloud. Students who did not receive their dendrite food notes back will understand that they may have missed part of the critical point. It is their job to rewrite dendrite food in their notebook or journal after listening to classmates read the best ones aloud.

If most students' summaries are incorrect, it is information to the teacher that the lesson may not have been as clear as intended and should be retaught in another manner to reach the objectives.

Exit cards. These are similar to dendrite food. Students write a brief summary of what they think the key point of the lesson was and hand it to the teacher as their exit card for leaving the room. If examination of the cards shows that, in general, students are missing the point, then the lesson needs reteaching. Good exit cards are posted for the class to read and saved for absent students to review when they return.

Assessing the Assessment Tools

Even with varied types of assessments, it is valuable to consider in advance how the results of those assessments will be used to benefit student understanding and teaching strategy success. Instead of giving a test, recording the grades for compilation in a report card, and moving on, consider the ways of collecting and reviewing assessment data:

• For informal observational assessments, predetermine what is being assessed on a particular day. Is it cooperative behavior, focus, amount of work done, study habits, problem-solving strategies, or final answers?

• Recording brief notes about exceptional work or cases of difficulty will provide prompts later for individual recognition, extra help, or class discussion about what went right and what went wrong.

• Formative assessment takes place when teachers make explicit efforts to link the results of their assessments to future learning. Data for this teacher self-assessment can come from any of the following:
   • Videotaping lessons
   • Colleague-peer observations of teaching
   • Triangulation—where teacher impression of what they think they taught, observer impression of what they believe was taught, and student report of what they learned can be eye-opening. Sometimes what one thinks was taught is not what the students learned. The triangulation data make this disconnect evident.

Tests for formative purposes are most valuable when they give students the opportunity to demonstrate more than rote memory. Problem-solving activities call upon the executive functions of judgment, critical analysis, evidence gathering, and clear communication.

When those are part of the assessment, even the process of solving the problem reinforces the learned material in cortical brain areas where it will be stored and becomes available to retrieve for subsequent higher cognitive activities.

Metacognition by the student after the assessment is useful. Students discover what was missing from their studying that resulted in gaps in their knowledge during the assessment. More important, they have the immediate reinforcement of realizing what they did right in their preparation so they can use those strategies again.

Assessment Preparation

Standardized testing is likely to be part of our educational system for some time. Students will do better on these tests when they have practiced with the format. A progression of test practice from comfortable settings through more realistic settings helps reduce stress and build test-taking comfort. Students can first practice standardized testing in low-stress classroom environments, for short periods, with breaks. Then students are told that the testing situation in the classroom will be changed so they can experience what it might feel like in the standardized test situation. These training sessions can incorporate strictly timed segments and use of the same type of answer sheets used for the standardized tests. If students know that these sessions are opportunities to practice the test-taking strategies they have learned and to experience the feelings of the testing situation, they will have reduced anxiety come test day.

These techniques do more than reduce the stress and anxiety that interfere with neuronal transmission of information through the affective filter. They also reduce the learner helplessness that results from perceived threat or fear of failure. Techniques to reduce test anxiety include the following:

1. After practice tests, let students correct their own papers, rather than experience the stress of switching papers. Provide clear explanations for the answers that are given and have students make corrections on their papers and take notes about what they need to study.

2. Always give adequate advance notice for all tests and quizzes so students don't develop test anxiety.

3. Before starting the test, have students visualize their successful performance. This visualization activates the memory circuits that will be called upon to solve the problems and answer the questions on the test. Just as visualizing a tennis swing or soccer kick can activate the critical brain networks, this successful test visualization will bring the brain circuits online.

4. A similar technique that pre-activates the necessary thinking centers of the brain before an exam is a *priming session* where students name things they think might be important to remember on the test. If these are written down on the board, the visual and auditory reminders reach these different style learners simultaneously. This priming is not the same as a review session that is held before test day. It is more of a brain pump-primer to bring the important information "online" in memory that they will use on the test.

5. Practice relaxing rituals immediately before tests, such as deep breathing or sensory relaxation, where students close their eyes and spend a few minutes sequentially relaxing the parts of their bodies. The teacher names the part to relax, beginning with the toes and going up to the chest, fingers, arms, neck, forehead, and eyes. When students are fully relaxed, the visualization of success can be a verbal suggestion made by the teacher.

6. Test destressors such as a funny or clever motto or saying included on the second page of the test can reduce tension. Allowing a stretch after 20 minutes or encouraging students to drink from their desk water bottles can serve the same purpose as syn-naps to restore the depleting supply of brain neurotransmitters.

7. Show students that incorrect answers on homework, quizzes, or tests do not mean they are poor learners. When they see that teachers make mistakes too and realize that all people can learn by correcting their mistakes, students realize that there is value in having their work corrected and graded, because that provides feedback so they too can learn from their mistakes.

8. Allow opportunities for making test corrections in preparation for retests. This correcting process builds students' knowledge banks, and the process of making corrections can increase metacognition.

a. For example, on a test correction sheet in math, the student is asked to find (and write down) the page number in the textbook where an example of the problem can be found and to review that example.

b. Next, the student describes the type of mistake (for example, was it an error in simple arithmetic addition or was it confusion about the concept of how to multiply negative numbers?).

c. After assessing where their understanding was incomplete, students should write what they will do to learn the material (such as meet with the teacher during study hall, review textbook examples before tests, or practice their multiplication tables).

d. This process shows students how to review text examples to study for future tests and gives them confidence in their ability to work through challenging problems on their own with the textbook as a resource. The result is a reduction in test anxiety and learned helplessness.

e. Students are motivated to do the test correction sheets because they know it is their key to being able to take a retest.

Assessments as Learning Experiences to Suit Individual Learning Styles

Most teachers and current textbooks offer varied approaches to the material to be learned so the teaching can be brain-compatible with varied student learning styles. It is only logical that respect for these individual learning styles be incorporated into assessment modalities.

For example, teachers responsive to interpersonal learning styles find cooperative group work a way to pull in those learners as well to give students with artistic, computer, dramatic, or organizational skills the opportunities to enter the learning experience, through their strengths and interests. It follows that assessments should also provide opportunities for each student's unique learning style to access his or her highest performance success level.

A variety of assessment modalities and some student choice in assessment type can bring students to the assessment with less anxiety and increase the positive learning experience, as well as provide the opportunity for them to demonstrate what they know and not simply what they memorized, forgot, or never learned. Examples include tests where notes or textbooks are permitted, take-home tests, and student-made tests that they prepare and the teacher can alter so that the answers are not just memorized. For example, in history, after studying the different agricultural products in the northern and southern colonies, the self-test questions a student writes might be these: What were the crops from the colonies in the north and from the south? How are the climates, land, and water supply different in one northern city and one southern city?

When the teacher rewrites the question, it could prompt more analysis and executive function connections if it is rephrased: "Give an example of how the climate, water supply, and soil influenced the agricultural products in one northern and one southern city during the Colonial Era." In this example, the teacher knows that the student has reviewed the facts necessary to make the higher-level connection and analysis and therefore has the tools for successful higher-level thinking.

This is the process I use for student-created math final exams:

• I give the structure for the tests that students are required to create, such as, "Include 15 calculations and 5 word problems with 2 from each of the 10 subsections of the chapter."

• I make a copy of each test and change the numbers, but not the structure of the equations. They know I will make these changes and that the numbers on their tests will be different than the ones they used.

• Students are assigned homework to make practice tests on their own, using the template of the test they created and changing the numbers themselves.

• In class, for further review, students exchange their practice tests with partners for study and to confirm the accuracy of their answers (I don't have an answer key to their self-created tests).

Projects (pre-approved by the teacher) that demonstrate comprehension or mastery of the material covered in the unit can be ideal assessments. They can become the packaging that connects the newly learned patterns of knowledge to related, previously stored knowledge. To see if a project demonstrates comprehension or mastery, consider these questions: Does this assessment examine understanding and not just rote memory? Is the student called upon to think during the creation of the project?

These projects can include skits, posters, oral presentations, debates, papers, or demonstrations that assess understanding apart from rote knowledge. For some units, the projects can be done in pairs or groups, as long as there is a means of assessing each individual student's participation in the final product. This assessment could be made through verbal interviews with students individually after the completion or presentation of the project.

A project example for a unit of study of modern Europe would have students select a country and simulate travel to that country, including finding out how to get passports and visas, what the passport oath is, what clothing to bring, what hotels are near the important historic or cultural places they plan to visit, the money exchange rate, a budget, location of cities to visit along their travel route through their country, useful phrases to know in that language, cultural behaviors appropriate to that country, or items they might expect to find on menus. They might also create a menu, write a travelogue, cook a meal, or prepare a "scrapbook" with pictures from the Internet and descriptions of their responses to "visits" they made to these places.

If standardized testing is of critical importance, each unit can include a test in that format to get students used to the experience. However, let them know that the more authentic assessment will be equal to or greater than the standardized test in terms of importance in their final grade. This will reduce test anxiety and show them that higher-level thinking and reasoning are valued more than rote memory in the big picture, but that they must be prepared to be successful on all types of assessments.

Assessment Accommodations for Students with ADD

Just as teaching students with learning differences means setting appropriately high, but not necessarily uniform, standards and expectations for speed of learning, assessing should also be differentiated. Especially considering the underdeveloped maturation of the frontal lobes of many students with ADD, it is unreasonable to have identical expectations for their frontal lobe executive function performance on assessments.

These students' brains may not do well with rote memorizing or even relational memory that is based on rote memorized patterns, algorithms, or abstractions such as, "When two vowels go walking, the first does the talking." More specific testing would be appropriate, such as looking at math problems with the solutions worked out and selecting which one is done correctly. They could match correctly spelled words with their meanings instead of having to memorize the definitions. Then they could have their tests returned with any mistakes clearly marked. For the matches they get wrong, they will then see the correct definition matched with the correct word and be required to use the word correctly in a sentence that clearly shows its meaning.

Toll the Death Knell for the Bell Curve

I taught for several years at a school where almost half of the students entering my 5th grade class had inadequate math preparation and told me that they were poor math students. "I'm just dumb at math," "I never get it," and "I hate math and it's my worst subject" were their literal comments. Their parents had similar predictions: "My daughter is creative and loves school but has never been good at math" or, "He just is bad at math and always has been. We'd like to start with a tutor right away."

Age 10 is much too young to determine anyone's academic potential, yet these children and adults were discouraged about math. Regardless of past academic experiences or the admonitions of previous teachers about students' deficiencies, it is critical that students be seen as potentially successful individuals and that teachers proceed optimistically with the brain-based strategies that can help them reach their potential.

As described earlier, emotional well-being and self-confidence set the ideal neurological state for brain encoding of data. The studies described confirmed the negative impact of stress on memory storage and the positive effect of dopamine release when students expect a positive experience. It follows that student expectations and confidence, as well as teacher bias based upon previous teachers' grades or test scores, are influential in ultimate student success.

Following the brain-based research, my goal was to first teach to these students' individual learning styles in a classroom community that provided low stress and supportive challenge. I realized that grades were important to these students and their families and that they were required for report cards. I wanted the grading system to be a positive incentive without being a source of stress and alienation from school. I instituted a policy of test correction sheets as a passport to retests.

My goal was for all students to be motivated to achieve mastery in each unit of study we covered. Often students in elementary school are tested at the end of the unit, and then the next unit is started regardless of the test results. Elementary arithmetic is critical if these children are to be successful in all future higher mathematics. Therefore, in my class, if they did not show mastery on a test by reaching at least 85 percent accuracy, I encouraged them to complete a test correction paper as their "ticket" to take a retest.

These correction papers were not simple. They were an exercise in metacognition, because the student was required to find the example in their text that matched the problem they got wrong and write that page number on their paper. They then were required to communicate in written words (creating a secondary, language-centered neuron network communicating with the math concept) what they should have done differently to solve the problem correctly.

Note that rather than have students write what they did wrong and possibly reinforce that erroneous material, they write what they should have done correctly. They next solved the problem or calculation correctly, getting help if needed. After they successfully solved the problems they got wrong the first time and proved their comprehension on the test correction page, they could take a retest, on which they inevitably were more successful in achieving mastery of the topic.

The end result was that students who once considered themselves math failures were willing to keep working because they experienced the direct correlation between practice and success. Their success was translated into the numbers and letter grades that reflected the mastery they authentically achieved.

At the same time I was using the test-correction approach, another teacher at the school was not only using grades as a source of comparing one student's success to another's, she was posting these grades on colorful bar graphs on the class Web site for all to see. Although students' names were not affixed to the reported scores, it was clear to students, their parents, and classmates where their scores ranked on those imposing bar graphs.

The difference in these two approaches to test results was emotionally profound. When students feel empowered to practice because they have had the experience that with continued effort they will achieve greater success, they will make the effort. When seeing their low status on bar graphs discouraged students, they often felt incompetent and hopeless. A longitudinal study of middle schoolers showed that teachers who emphasize competitive comparisons of student ability discourage students from asking for help (Ryan, 1998).

With competitive grading, it is understandable that the neuro-*logical* brain response is negativity and resistance to further learning due to the heightened metabolism in the blocking affective filter. At one point, an administrator chastised me saying that my students' math grades were "inflated" because there was not a bell-curve *C* to coincide with each *A* my students received.

Bell-curve statistical analysis might hold true for population dynamics and other large data sampling of random large groups over time, but it does not belong in a place where students need encouragement and positive reinforcement. Especially in grades K–8, where class ranking does not affect college placement, educators best serve all their students when they provide opportunities for mastery-related success rather than bell curve graphs.

Grades on routine written tests may be useful as measures of one aspect of quantitative rote or working memory of the subject material.

They may provide one measure to help determine student assignment to ability groups or levels of high school course challenge. However, in grades K–8, the emphasis on traditional testing as the primary means of student-to-student comparison on bar graphs and bell curves results in needless loss of confidence and raising of their affective filters. These graphs reduce the complexity of children's multiple intelligences to one measurement. Using one type of assessment as the determination of students' achievement is as illogical as suggesting that height is the defining factor of athletic skill.

When the goal is to discover what students have mastered after appropriate teaching, the bell curve does not ring true. Having a low end that is an equal match of the high end gives the message that half the students will perform up to, but not beyond, a midpoint. Students are responsive to teacher expectations, so why restrict those expectations by imposing an artificial bell curve (Rosenthal & Jacobson, 1992)?

 Gray Matter

An analysis by Jonathan Fife (1999) described the inaccuracies in using bell curve analysis to judge students. He reviewed experimental data where teachers were told that they were being assigned high-achieving students, but actually were assigned a random cross section. Nevertheless, these students completed the year with the best performance on the standardized tests.

Fife used this experiment to demonstrate the power of having a belief that students will be successful. Even though it was not associated with neuroimaging scans, it is consistent with the subsequent fMRI and PET scan data that positive self-image and high comfort and confidence levels are associated with more efficient encoding of new information and more successful patterning and long-term memory storage of that material.

Fife also suggested that there is a difference between believing that all students can exceed their potential and expecting that only a few will be very successful as is dictated by a bell curve. His reasonable interpretation was that this and similar studies demonstrated that, more often than not, students will have high performance if allowed to and that high expectations give students permission to be exceptional.

In his opinion, expecting the bell curve to be the model of performance gives only a very few students permission to excel. It was Fife's experience that grading on the curve was an acknowledgment that a teacher does not know how to assess students' knowledge in a course, so he or she uses the curve to minimize the chance of grading error by controlling for too many high and low grades. Another correlation of teachers who rely on curves to determine grades that Fife reported was that those teachers tended not to have clearly identified objectives for what a student should be learning and what knowledge represents an *A* level of proficiency. They also often failed to make that differentiation clear to their students.

Fife considered the final tragedy of grading on a curve to be the teachers who judge their success by how many of their students receive high grades. Because of the statistics of the bell curve, there is an upper limit of students who can receive high grades. The truth is that a teacher who gives most students an *A* may not be guilty of grade inflation but may be an outstanding teacher, because all the students deserved and received *A* grades for *A* competency. He concluded that grading needs to rethought and designed to maintain standards while at the same time promoting high expectations for all students (Fife, 1999).

Teacher Response to Student Achievement

Assessment is usually something teachers think of in terms of tests, projects, reports, or other evidence of learning or effort over time. That is true for most assessments that teachers structure for record keeping or analysis of the learning of a unit of study. From the student perspective, it may appear that teachers are critically judging them from moment to moment during the class—and watching for them to make mistakes, rather than looking for their comprehension. In fact, when students are asked about what they think their teachers think about them or their work, they frequently interpret tone of voice, facial expression, and teacher mood as directly reflecting the teacher's feelings about—or assessment of—them and their work.

If students give teachers this much status when there is no specifically directed or intended criticism, imagine how words of praise or correction can affect students. Regardless of their façade, students do feel the sting of what they interpret as criticism as well as the pride of what they believe is positive teacher response to their comments, clothes, posture, actions, homework, tests, verbal responses, or questions. That is a very powerful position of influence for teachers. With the knowledge we now have about how emotions alter brain chemistry and neuronal data processing, it is important to use that power wisely.

Just as the endorphins and dopamine released by pleasurable activity or exercise are released to all parts of the brain, the epinephrine (adrenaline) pumped out during times of excitement or stress also has generalized impact. For children and adolescents, their impressions of what their teachers think of them at any point in time can be reflected in their brain chemistry. When their impressions of teacher opinion affect their emotions, there are reflected changes in their brains' release of hormones and neurotransmitters, resulting in mood and behavior responses.

The research on teacher praise or recognition from the 1970s to the early 1990s led to theories that praise was a form of extrinsic reward and as such decreased student motivation. The assumption was that the extrinsic reward of teacher praise would reduce student motivation to strive for the self-satisfaction of intrinsic reward for jobs they believed were well done (Kohn, 1993). Subsequent meta-analysis of these studies revealed that they were measuring student use of *free time* as the evidence for their loss of intrinsic motivation (Wiersma, 1992).

Subsequent studies, measuring multiple criteria for intrinsic motivation revealed that *effective* teacher recognition has positive correlation to student motivation as measured by the brain's dopamine-reward cycle on scans and neurochemical analysis. Therefore, effective praise is a useful tool in motivating student effort and achievement (Cameron & Pierce, 1994). The characteristics of effective praise include the following:

• **Predictability.** Students must understand the circumstances or actions that will result in praise—rubrics are helpful tools in providing predictable parameters of expectations.

• **Specificity.** Students know the particulars of what they accomplished to merit recognition. Instead of simply telling a student, "Your painting is pretty," make the comment specific by saying, "You blended colors well to show that the sun was setting."

• **Comparison should not be competitive.** Compare students to their own previous work to acknowledge improvement: "You seem to understand least common denominators much better now, and it shows in the way you can add fractions." Students must never feel tricked by evaluation processes or that the standards have been lowered so their work could be praised. It is better to wait for authentic success than to give superficial praise for a student's mediocre work.

• **Praise for effort.** Praise that explicitly acknowledges the connection between the students' additional effort and their specific achievement, rather than praise for intelligence, causes them to work more, experience more enjoyment, and be more persistent in tasks (Mueller & Dweck, 1998).

Effective Communication of Assessment Results to Students

Even when the assessment is a traditional test or graded paper or project, it is best to avoid handing the work back to students during class, when there will be the inevitable boasting about good grades, crumpling of low-grade papers, and worst of all, little or no attention paid to the teacher comments diligently written on the papers. The ideal is to return important student assessments when individual conferring is possible. This conferring can occur when the class is engaged in independent individual or cooperative group work or during office hours, lunch, or break, when students can be seen individually.

A private assessment conference can build skills and competency when accurate reinforcement and feedback are compassionately delivered. Growth of learning and thinking skills takes place during the process of introspection and self-awareness. When there is a problem that students can identify without fear, they are mentally prepared to process the learning experience, rather than becoming emotionally blocked to constructive suggestions.

When they are not blocked by stress or anxiety and believe they can improve their academic success by following suggestions, students are ready for helpful advice. If they are too emotional initially, it is best to reassure them that the meeting can be held later in the day, or on the following day, and to let them know that they still have the opportunity to succeed.

When the conference takes place, helping students use metacognition will facilitate their acknowledging what they did right to be successful. If they are not satisfied with their performance, what are their goals, and how do they think they can achieve them?

What are realistic versus optimistic goals for students? The most memorable engraving for me at Williams College was the encouragement to "Aim High—Aim Far, Your Goal the Sun, Your Aim the Stars." As noted in the Rosenthal and Jacobson research and supported by the past decade of brain imaging, teachers can combine the best of their professional art with the brain research about learning to let students aim for the stars, while helping them place their suns within their grasp for individualized achievement goals.

Teachers who change lives help students envision and achieve realistic goals without limiting their dreams. If students' expectations seem unrealistic, these teachers reassure them that starting with the first goal of the sun does not mean that the stars are impossible. In fact, the sun is a star, and can someday be a jumping-off point to those other stars.

The most valuable assessment conferences do the following:

• Prompt students to believe they can improve.

• Motivate them to want to acquire the tools or study habits that they trust will result in that improvement.

• In the post-assessment conferences, students' confidence about and investment in the plan they develop with teachers is intensified when they write it down.

• There is further validation of students' potential to succeed if they then formalize their plan into a written contract that can be signed by the student, their parents, and the teacher.

• When students read the contract, especially when there are additional comments of support and confidence from their teacher, they believe they are capable of success with effort and that their teacher is committed to helping them achieve that success.

What Teachers Can Learn from Assessments

Once conventional assessments are completed, traditional teachers move on to the next unit. Alternatively, if the assessment data are viewed as a measure of how well the unit was taught, there is the opportunity to discover which teaching strategies worked and which need revision.

Rubrics for teacher self-assessment can be created at the start of a unit, with categories such as the following:

• Student engagement
• Opportunities for varied learning styles
• Opportunities for some student choice

• Student success as measured on standardized tests as well as on problem-solving or other executive function assessments

• Student self-assessment

Ideally, teachers can write notes in the designated rubric categories during and after the teaching of the unit. Additional notes that are added after the final student assessments and feedback provide insights that might not otherwise be evident. When these steps are followed, the resulting self-assessments empower teachers to design future instruction to better meet the needs of all students.

AFTERWORD:
THE FUTURE IS NOW

To keep our faces toward change and behave like free spirits in the presence of fate is strength undefeatable.

~ Helen Keller

We are at an exciting and challenging crossroads in education. Science, especially neuroimaging, is giving us real-time visual images of how the brain learns and which teaching strategies most successfully affect the learning process. There is also the challenge of partisan elected officials' interest in using educational funding and programs as political capital to manipulate voters. We are in the technological, instant-gratification phase of public assessment of educational programs, with parents and voters looking at teachers, administrators, and curriculum developers to fix the societal problems that are mirrored in some classrooms. As illogical as that blame game is, educators need to be armed to defend our areas of expertise. The dismal alternative would be an educational system dominated by the agendas of partisan politicians or groups with financial interests.

Howard Gardner wrote in *The Futurist,* a Harvard educational journal (2000) that "if schools do not change rapidly and radically, they are likely to be replaced by other, more responsive institutions." I prefer to be more optimistic, along the lines of Charles Darwin's theory: "It is not the strongest species that survives, nor the most intelligent, but the ones most responsive to change."

I don't believe the only answer is in Gardner's "rapid and radical" change, but rather a well-planned response using the new information derived from the neuroscience of learning. That is why Helen Keller's wisdom of keeping our faces toward change and behaving like the informed, independent thinkers we are is what will give strength to our voices as educators.

If this book was helpful in providing strategies based on brain research that will apply to your classrooms or schools, you are now more empowered by the science of education to help students reach their best academic potential. Next, just as the poor family living near the ocean is helped more by learning how to fish than by being given fish to eat, you will build educational muscle from learning how to interpret the validity of "brain research" of the future.

Not all studies claiming to be "brain-based" are valid, and there is no authenticating agency that must approve the claims of self-proclaimed educational experts. The U.S. Food and Drug Administration (FDA) must approve new prescription medications for both effectiveness and safety, but there is no such watchdog agency to scrutinize educational claims.

Many of the same criteria that apply to the validity of medical research can be used to evaluate the soundness of educational studies. In medicine, we consider the size of the subject group critical. There must also be a double-blind protocol, where the investigators and the subjects do not know if they are in a control group or the experimental group receiving the drug or therapy being studied. The subjects must be randomly placed in the two groups, the results of the research need to be reproducible by other investigators using the same medication or treatment, and all variables must be controlled.

Because there is no FDA to supervise clinical trials, safety, and effectiveness of educational theories and products, educators need to be their own analysts. By asking questions and requesting research data to see if the educational theory or product has been tested in large studies with control groups and unbiased data analysts, you put the burden of proof on the person or group pitching the product or strategy. Anecdotal stories about techniques that have changed students' lives show ideal outcomes. Just like weight loss testimonials, individual results can be quite variable, so statistical analysis of large groups of students becomes critical.

It is not too difficult for unscrupulous "educational technique" pitchmen to misrepresent their products. Scientific research is by its evolving nature tentative and transient; scientific investigation is always re-evaluating data, especially when more sophisticated tools of measurement become available. Until we had radio telescopes with greater precision and reach, the available evidence indicated that Neptune was always closer to Earth than Pluto. With better tools of measurement, it was found that Pluto's orbit is elliptical in shape, so at times Pluto travels closer to the sun than Neptune's orbit. This phenomenon was the case from January 1979 through February 1999, when Neptune was the farthest planet from the sun.

Scientific research is continuously evolving as technology and precision of measurement improves and researchers have more experience with the data. The scientific and medical communities realize that when data are subject to interpretation, more precise technology will lead to more refined and specific results. Nonscientists, especially partisan politicians or corporations with vested interest in a particular curriculum or government-endorsed education policy, can take unscrupulous advantage of the changeability in scientific research results to misread data as support for their vested interests. There have been biased interpretations of phonics-heavy reading instruction released by the companies that finance the curriculum packages and the appointed partisan government commissions that recommend them.

In our era of evidence-based education, objective scientific evidence provided by brain imaging studies has reduced our reliance on philosophy or opinion. In considering a teaching strategy, when educators ask if there is scientific evidence that the program is effective, students are protected from unproven programs. Awareness of new scientific knowledge puts educators in the rightful position of insisting that programs used in their schools reflect what is known about the science of learning and effective learning strategies that are compatible with brain research.

Brain research, when applied to the classroom, can not only drive the learning process but also allow teachers to energize and enliven the minds of students. As the research continues to build, it will be the challenge of educators to develop and use new strategies that bring the fruits of the research to the students in our classrooms. That will be a fascinating and exciting challenge to meet. The more educators learn about the structure and function of the brain, the more prepared we will be to meet that challenge.

GLOSSARY

Acetylcholine: A neurotransmitter that stimulates multiple brain centers, including the hippocampus, brainstem, and forebrain (where new learning takes place).

ACTH: A cortisone-releasing hormone that has a positive alerting effect. It is released in response to surprise, novelty, and personal associations. When these feelings are linked to new learning, the released ACTH promotes growth of new dendrites and synaptic connections between neurons. This creates additional circuits and connections between the new information.

Affective Filter: Refers to an emotional state of stress in students during which they are not responsive to processing, learning, and storing new information. This affective filter is represented by objective physical evidence on neuroimaging of the amygdala, which becomes metabolically hyperactive during periods of high stress. In this hyperstimulated state, new information does not pass through the amygdala to reach the information processing centers of the brain.

Amygdala: Part of the limbic system in the brain's temporal lobe. It was first believed to function as a brain center for responding only to anxiety and fear. When the amygdala senses threat, it becomes overactivated (high metabolic activity as seen by greatly increased radioactive glucose and oxygen use in the amygdala region on PET and fMRI scans). In students, these neuroimaging findings are seen when they feel helpless and anxious. When the amygdala is in this state of stress, fear, or anxiety-induced overactivation, new information coming through the sensory intake areas of the brain cannot pass through the amygdala's affective filter to gain access to the memory circuits.

Awareness: Attention of the moment.

Brain Mapping: Using electroencephalographic (EEG) response over time, brain mapping measures electrical activity representing brain activation along neural pathways. This technique allows scientists to track what parts of the brain are active when a person is processing information at various stages of information intake, patterning, storing, and retrieval. The levels of activation in particular brain regions are associated with the intensity of information processing.

Broca's Language Center: For over 90 percent of people, this language-processing center for the motor control of speech is in the left frontal lobe near the hippocampus.

Calpain: This enzyme breaks down cells with excess calcium ions. Cells require blood to bring nourishment and clear away waste such as excess calcium. Underactivated cells don't send messages to the circulatory system to send blood. This reduced blood flow means that calcium ions that accumulate around the cell are not washed away. This calcium ion build-up triggers the secretion of the enzyme calpain, which causes cells to self-destruct. This is a proposed mechanism in the pruning destruction of brain cells that are not used in the "use it or lose it" phenomenon.

Cerebellar Stimulation: A theory proposed for increasing development in the underdeveloped frontal lobes of some people with ADD/ADHD. The theory proposes that physical exercises that call on the balance and coordination centers in the cerebellum in the back of the brain will stimulate the frontal lobes. The theory is based on the finding that almost half of the brain's neurons are found in the cerebellum and many of them have connections with the frontal lobes. It is proposed, though not proven, that increased cerebellar stimulation increases the stimulation and maturation of cortical neurons in the frontal lobes.

Chunking: Because the working memory has a capacity for immediate recall limited to from five to nine pieces of unrelated items, if information is separated into chunks of that size, students can remember it more successfully.

Computerized Tomography (CT Scan, CAT Scan): This scan uses a narrow beam of X-rays to create brain images displayed as a series of brain slices. A computer program estimates how much of the beam is absorbed in small areas within cross sections of the brain to produce the image.

Decoding Sensory Input: Any new information or learning must enter the brain through one or more of the senses (hearing, seeing/visualizing, touching, tasting, smelling, and emotionally feeling). First, the information is decoded by the sense's specific sensory receptors in the body. From there the information travels through the nerves in the skin or body to the spinal cord and up through the reticular activating system to the specialized part of the brain that interprets (decodes) the input from the particular senses.

Dendrite Food: A nickname for a student activity summarizing new information in their own words and recording these notes labeled as "dendrite food." This phrase refers to the fact that new learning, when it is physically established in the brain, is accompanied by the growth of more connections between nerve cells called dendrites.

Dendrites: Branched protoplasmic extensions that sprout from the arms (axons) or the cell bodies of neurons. Dendrites conduct electrical impulses toward the neighboring neurons. A single nerve may possess many dendrites. Dendrites increase in size and number in response to learned skills, experience, and information storage. New dendrites grow as branches from frequently activated neurons. Proteins called neurotrophins, such as nerve growth factor, stimulate this dendrite growth.

Dopamine: A neurotransmitter most associated with attention, decision making, executive function, and reward-stimulated learning. Using neuroimaging, dopamine release has been found to increase in response to rewards and positive experiences. Scans reveal greater dopamine release while subjects are playing, laughing, exercising, and receiving acknowledgment (e.g., praise) for achievement.

EEG (Electroencephalogram): EEG measures the electrical activity occurring from transmissions between neurons in the cerebral cortex.

Endorphins: Peptide hormones that bind to opiate receptors found mainly in the brain. When endorphins activate these receptors, the effect may naturally mimic the opiate (narcotic) effect of reducing the sensation of pain and increasing pleasant emotions. Increased endorphin release is associated with pleasurable activity and exercise.

Episodic Memory: This autobiographical memory is the explicit memory of events such as time, place, and associated emotions that occur together. These are usually associated with single exposures to an experience or life episode that are later recalled in multisensory detail.

Event Memories: Memories tied to specific emotionally or physically charged events (strong sensory input). Memory theory suggests that memory-provoking or dramatic events can be linked to academic information to increase the emotional significance of the information and thereby increase its memory storage. Recalling the associated emotionally significant event with which academic information is connected (such as by surprise) may prompt subsequent recollection of the academic material when the event is recalled.

Executive Function: Cognitive processing of information that takes place in areas in the left frontal lobe and prefrontal cortex that exercise conscious control over one's emotions and thoughts. This control allows for patterned information to be used for organizing, analyzing, sorting, connecting, planning, prioritizing, sequencing, self-monitoring, self-correcting, assessment, abstractions, problem solving, attention focusing, and linking information to appropriate actions.

Flashbulb Memories: Powerful emotional events may be remembered in great detail following a highly personally significant event. These flashbulb memories result in powerful associative memories, such as what we were doing at the time we heard or saw the event. Critics of this theory contend that flashbulb memories are no more likely to be remembered than ordinary memories, but are more vividly recalled because people discuss (review) these significant events more frequently.

Frontal Lobes: With respect to learning, the frontal lobes contain the centers of executive function that organize and arrange information and coordinate the production of language and the focusing of attention.

Functional Brain Imaging (Neuroimaging): The use of techniques to directly or indirectly demonstrate the structure, function, or biochemical status of the brain. *Structural* imaging reveals the overall structure of the brain, and *functional* neuroimaging provides visualization of the processing of sensory information coming to the brain and of commands going from the brain to the body. This processing is visualized directly as areas of the brain "lit up" by increased metabolism, blood flow, oxygen use, or glucose uptake. Functional brain imaging reveals neural activity in particular brain regions as the brain performs discrete cognitive tasks.

Functional Magnetic Resonance Imaging (fMRI): This type of functional brain imaging uses the paramagnetic properties of oxygen-carrying hemoglobin in the blood to demonstrate which brain structures are activated and to what degree during various performance and cognitive activities. Most fMRI-scan learning research has subjects scanned while they are exposed to visual, auditory, or tactile stimuli and then reveals the brain structures that are activated by these experiences (exposures).

Gray Matter: This term refers to the brownish-gray color of the nerve cell bodies and dendrites of the brain and spinal cord (in contrast to white matter, which is primarily composed of supportive tissue).

Hippocampus: A ridge in the floor of each lateral ventricle of the brain that consists mainly of gray matter and that has a major role in memory processes. The hippocampus takes sensory inputs and integrates them with relational or associational patterns, thereby binding the separate aspects of the experience into storable patterns of relational memories.

Hypothalamus: The part of the brain that lies below the thalamus and regulates body temperature, certain metabolic processes, and other autonomic activities that maintain the body at homeostasis (steady physiological state).

Limbic System: A group of interconnected deep brain structures involved in olfaction (smell), emotion, motivation, behavior, and various autonomic functions. Included in the limbic system are the thalamus, amygdala, hippocampus, and portions of the frontal and temporal lobes. If the limbic system becomes overstimulated by stress-provoking emotion (seen as very high metabolic activity lighting up those brain areas), the information taught at that time will be poorly transmitted or stored in the long-term memory centers.

Medial Temporal Lobe (MTL): The regions on the inner side of each temporal lobe that connect with the prefrontal cortex in a circuit. The MTL binds the separate elements of an experience into an integrated memory. This area of the brain includes several areas that are critical for new memory formation, including the hippocampus.

Metabolic Hyperstimulation: The increased metabolism (biologic use) of oxygen or glucose to fuel nerve cells is demonstrated on functional scans. For example, when the amygdala is in its highly metabolic state of hyperstimulation from stress, the pathways through the amygdala leading to memory storage are blocked. When these pathways are blocked by the hypermetabolic amygdala, scans reveal a lack of metabolic activity in the centers of reasoning and long-term memory beyond the amygdala. In other words, when the limbic system, particularly the amygdala, is hyperstimulated by high stress, it becomes flooded by so much neural metabolic activity that new information cannot pass through it to memory storage and reasoning parts of the brain.

Metacognition: Knowledge about one's own information processing and strategies that influence one's learning that can optimize future learning. After a lesson or assessment, when students are prompted to recognize the successful learning strategies that they used, that reflection can reinforce the effective strategies.

Neuronal Circuits: Neurons communicate with each other by sending coded messages along electrochemical connections. When there is repeated stimulation of specific patterns of stimulation between the same group of neurons, their connecting circuit becomes more developed and more accessible to efficient stimulation and response. This is where practice (repeated stimulation of grouped neuronal connections in neuronal circuits) results in more successful recall.

Neurons: Specialized cells in the brain and throughout the nervous system that conduct electrical impulses to, from, and within the brain. Neurons are composed of a main cell body, a single axon for outgoing electrical signals, and a varying number of dendrites for incoming signals in electrical form.

Neurotransmitters: Brain proteins that are released by the electrical impulses on one side of the synapse to then float across the synaptic gap carrying the information with them to stimulate the next nerve ending in the pathway. Once the neurotransmitter is taken up by the next nerve ending, the electric impulse is reactivated to travel along to the next nerve. Neurotransmitters in the brain include serotonin, tryptophan, acetylcholine, dopamine, and others that transport information across synapses. When neurotransmitters are depleted by too much information traveling through a nerve circuit without a break, the speed of transmission along the nerve slows down to a less efficient level.

Neurotrophins (Nerve Growth Factor): Proteins that stimulate growth of nerve cells. During sleep, neurotrophins are released in greater amounts, and there is associate increase in the formation of new dendrites branching between neurons.

Occipital Lobes (Visual Memory Areas): These posterior lobes of the brain process optical input, among other functions.

Parietal Lobes: Parietal lobes on each side of the brain process sensory data, among other functions.

Patterning: Patterning is the process whereby the brain perceives sensory data and generates patterns by relating new with previously learned material or by chunking material into pattern systems it has used before. Education is about increasing the patterns students can use, recognize, and communicate. As the ability to see and work with patterns expands, the executive functions are enhanced. Whenever new material is presented in such a way that students see relationships, they can generate greater brain cell activity (formation of new neural connections) and achieve more successful patterns for long-term memory storage and retrieval.

Plasticity: Dendrite formation and dendrite and neuron destruction (pruning) allows the brain to reshape and reorganize the networks of dendrite-neuron connections in response to increased or decreased use of these pathways.

Positron Emission Tomography (PET Scans): Radioactive isotopes are injected into the blood attached to molecules of glucose. As a part of the brain becomes more active, its glucose and oxygen demands increase. The isotopes attached to the glucose give off measurable emissions used to produce maps of areas of brain activity. The higher the radioactivity count, the greater the activity taking place in that portion of the brain. PET scanning can show blood flow and oxygen and glucose metabolism in the tissues of the working brain that reflect the amount of brain activity in these regions while the brain is processing information or sensory input. The biggest drawback of PET scanning is that because the radioactivity decays rapidly, it is limited to monitoring short tasks. Newer fMRI technology does not have this same time limitation and has become the preferred functional imaging technique in learning research.

Prefrontal Cortex: The front part of the brain's frontal lobe, which responds to event and memory processing.

Pruning: Neurons are pruned (destroyed) when they are not used. In a baby, the brain overproduces brain cells (neurons) and connections between brain cells (synapses) and then starts pruning them back around the age of 3. The second wave of synapse formation occurs just before puberty and is followed by another phase of pruning. Pruning allows the brain to consolidate learning by pruning away unused neurons and synapses and wrapping white matter (myelin) around the neuronal networks more frequently used to stabilize and strengthen them.

Quantitative Electroencephalography (qEEG; Brain Mapping): This brain wave monitoring provides brain-mapping data based on the very precise localization of brain wave patterns coming from the parts of the brain actively engaged in the processing of information. Quantitative EEG uses digital technology to record electrical patterns at the surface of the scalp that represent cortical electrical activity or brain waves. "Functional" qEEG testing adds recording to evaluate the brain's responses to reading, listening, math, or other demands and to provide visual summaries in topographic maps.

Quickwrite Rubric Alternatives: A method of having students put down their thoughts without stopping for grammar, spelling, punctuation, or even to think before writing. Students think for one minute and write nonstop for two to three minutes about a specified topic. These quickwrites can then be used as prompts for further writing about the topic.

Reinforcement Learning Theories: Theories (such as Dopamine Reward Learning) based on the assumption that the brain finds some states of stimulation to be more desirable than others and makes associations between specific cues and these desirable states or goals.

REM Sleep: The "dream sleep" associated with rapid eye movement (REM). It is during non-REM sleep that memory storage is most efficient. This non-REM sleep period is when the brain transforms recent memories into long-term memories by building and extending the dendritic branches. This hard-wiring of information learned during the day results in stored memories.

Reticular Activating System (RAS): This lower part of the posterior brain filters all incoming stimuli and makes the "decision" as to what people attend or ignore. The RAS alerts the brain to sensory input that sense receptors in the body send up the spinal cord. The main categories that focus the attention of the RAS and, therefore, the student include physical need, choice, and novelty.

Rote Memory: This type of "memorization" is usually the most commonly required memory task for students in primary and secondary school. This type of learning involves "memorizing," and soon forgetting, facts that are often of little primary interest or emotional value to the student, such as a list of words. Facts that are memorized by rehearsing over and over and that don't have obvious or engaging patterns or connections are being processed by rote memory. With nothing to give them context or relationship to each other or to the student's lives, these facts are stored in remoter areas of the brain. These isolated bits are more difficult to locate and retrieve later because there are fewer nerve pathways leading to these remote storage systems.

Serotonin: A neurotransmitter used to carry messages between neurons. Too little serotonin may be a cause of depression. Dendritic branching is enhanced by the serotonin secreted by the brain predominantly between the sixth and eighth hour of sleep (non-REM).

Somatosensory Cortexes: One in each parietal brain lobe where input from each individual sense (hearing, touch, taste, vision, smell) is ultimately processed.

SPECT (Single Photon Emission Computed Tomography) Scans: Injected gamma ray–emitting radioisotopes reach the brain, and a gamma camera records data that a computer uses to construct two- or three-dimensional images of active brain regions. SPECT tracers are considered to be more limited and of lower resolution than PET scans.

Survival Level of Attention: Ideally, students are beyond a basic survival mode and can direct attention to more than just avoiding danger. However, too much stress can push them into this survival mode. This can occur when students feel confused and overwhelmed by a classroom experience such that they cannot connect with, focus on, or create patterns and meaning from a lesson's sensory input data.

Synapse: These gaps between nerve endings are where neurotransmitters like dopamine carry information across the space separating the axon extensions of one neuron from the dendrite that leads to the next neuron in the pathway. Before and after crossing the synapse as a chemical message, information is carried in an electrical state as it travels down the nerve.

Temporal Lobes: These lobes on the sides of the brain process auditory and verbal input, language and phonetic discrimination, mood stability through projection fibers leading to the limbic system, and learning.

Thalamus: The thalamus processes the original sensory input and determines if it will be kept in the temporary awareness portion of memory or be given more sustained attention. If it is processed as more than transient awareness, sensory input is passed along through the thalamus to the neurons in the amygdala.

Wernicke's Language Center: An area in the posterior temporal lobe, usually in the left hemisphere, involved in the recognition of spoken words.

Working Memory (Short-Term Memory): This memory can hold and manipulate information for use in the immediate future. Information is only held in working memory for about a minute. The memory working span of young adults (less in children and older adults) is approximately seven for digits, six for letters, and five for words.

Zone of Proximal Development (ZPD): Lev Vygotsky's "zone of readiness," including the actions or topics a student is ready to learn. The zone of proximal development is the gap between a learner's current or actual level of development and his or her potential level of development. This is the set of knowledge that the learner does not yet understand but has the ability to learn with guidance.

BIBLIOGRAPHY

Alexopoulou, E., & Driver, R. (1996). Small-group discussion in physics: Peer interaction modes in pairs and fours. *Journal of Research in Science Teaching, 33*(10), 1099–1114.

Andreasen, N. C., O'Leary, D. S., Paradiso, S., Cizadlo, T., Arndt, S., Watkins, G. L., et al. (1999). The cerebellum plays a role in conscious episodic memory retrieval. *Human Brain Mapping, 8*(4), 226–234.

Antil, L., Jenkins, J., & Watkins, S. (1998). Cooperative learning: Prevalence, conceptualizations, and the relation between research and practice. *American Educational Research Journal, 35*(3), 419–454.

Ashby, C. R., Thanos, P. K., Katana, J. M., Michaelides, E. L., Gardner, C. A., & Heidbreder, N. D. (1999). The selective dopamine antagonist. *Pharmacology, Biochemistry and Behavior, 81*(1), 190–197.

Bandura, A., & Schunk, D. H. (1981). Cultivating competence, self-efficacy, and intrinsic interest through proximal self-motivation. *Journal of Personality and Social Psychology, 41,* 568–578.

Bangert–Downs, R. L., Kulik, C. C., Kulick, J. A., & Morgan, M. (1991). The instructional effects of feedback in test-like events. *Review of Educational Research, 61*(2), 213–238.

Bernard, B. (1991). *Moving toward a just and vital culture: Multiculturalism in our schools.* Portland, OR: Northwest Regional Educational Laboratory.

Bjorkland, D. F., & Brown, R. D. (1998). Physical play and cognitive development: Integrating activity, cognition, and education. *Child Development, 69*(3), 604–606.

Black, J. E., Isaacs, K. R., Anderson, B. J., Alcantara, A. A., & Greenough, W. T. (1990). Learning causes synaptogenesis in cerebral cortex of adult rats. *Proceedings of the National Academy of Science, 87,* 5568–5572.

Bliss, T. V. P., & Collinridge, G. L. (1993). A synaptic model of memory: Long-term potentiation in the hippocampus. *Nature, 361,* 31–39.

Boggiano, A. (1993). Use of techniques promoting students' self-determination: Effects on students' analytic problem-solving skills. *Motivation and Emotion, 17,* 319–336.

Brewer, J., Zhao, Z., Desmond, J., Glover, G., & Gabrieli, J. (1998). Making memories: Brain activity that predicts how well visual experience will be remembered. *Science, 281*(5380), 1185–1187.

Brophy, J. (1981). Teacher praise: A functional analysis. *Review of Educational Research, 51,* 5–32.

Bull, B. L., & Wittrock, M. C. (1973). Imagery in the learning of verbal definitions. *British Journal of Educational Psychology, 43,* 289–293.

Calonico, J., & Calonico, B. (1972). Classroom interaction: A sociological approach. *Journal of Educational Research, 66*(4), 165–169.

Cameron, J., & Pierce, W. D. (1994). Reinforcement, reward, and intrinsic motivation: A meta–analysis. *Review of Educational Research, 64*(93), 363–422.

Chen, Z. (1999). Schema induction in children's analogical problem solving. *Journal of Educational Psychology, 91*(4), 703–715.

Christianson, S. A. (1992). Emotional stress and eyewitness memory: A critical review. *Psychological Bulletin, 112*(2), 284–309.

Chugani, H., (1998). Biological basis of emotions: Brain systems and brain development. *Pediatrics, 102,* 1225–1229.

Chugani, H. T., & Phelps, M. E. (1991). Imaging human brain development with positron emission tomography. *Journal of Nuclear Medicine, 32*(1), 23–26.

Cohen, E. (1986). *Designing groupwork: Strategies for the heterogeneous classroom.* New York: Teachers College Press.

Cottle, M. (2005, March 11). That's life: Media glare. *The New Republic.*

Coward, L. A. (1990). *Pattern thinking.* New York: Praeger.

Diamond, M., & Hopson, J. (1998). *Magic trees of the mind.* New York: Dutton

Dozier, R., Jr. (1998). *Fear itself.* New York: St. Martin's Press.

Druyan, S. (1997). Effects of the kinesthetic conflict on promoting scientific reasoning. *Journal of Research in Science Teaching, 34*(10), 1083–1099.

Duman, M. (1999). Neural plasticity to stress and antidepressant treatment. *Biological Psychiatry, 46*(9), 1181–1191.

Dunston, P. J. (1992). A critique of graphic organizer research. *Reading Research and Instruction, 31*(2), 57–65.

Durkin, K. (1995). *Developmental social psychology.* Cambridge, MA: Blackwell.

Eich, E. (1995). Searching for mood dependent memory. *Psychological Science, 6,* 67–75.

Erikson, E. (1968). *A way of looking at things.* International Encyclopedia of the Social Sciences, New York: Crowell–Collier, 286–292.

Fife, J. (1999). Response to Pygmalion in the classroom or Pygmalion as an example of the quality principles. *The National Teaching and Learning Forum, 8*(4).

Flick, L. (1992). Where concepts meet percepts. Stimulating analogical thought in children. *Science and Education, 75*(2), 215–230.

Frank, M., Issa, N., & Stryker, M. (2001). Sleep enhances plasticity in the developing visual cortex. *Neuron, 30*(1), 275–297.

Fuchs, J. L., Montemayor, M., & Greenough, W. T. (1990). Effect of environmental complexity on size of the superior colliculus. *Behavioral and Neural Biology, 54*(2), 198–203.

Gabrieli, J. (2000). New terrain: Mapping the human brain. *Neuron, 25*(2), 493–500.

Gates, B. (2005). Prepared remarks for the National Education Summit on High Schools. Retrieved April 10, 2006, from the Bill and Melinda Gates Foundation Web site: http://www.gatesfoundation.org/MediaCenter/Speeches/BillgSpeeches/BGSpeechNGA–050226.htm.

Gerlic, I., & Jausovec, N. (1999). Multimedia: Differences in cognitive processes observed with EEG. *Educational Technology Research and Development, 47*(3), 5–14.

Giedd, J., Blumenthal, J., Jeffries, N., Castellanos, F., Liu, H., Zijdenbos, A., et al. (1999). Brain development during childhood and adolescence: A longitudinal MRI study. *Nature Neuroscience, 2*: 861–863.

Giedd, J. N., Gogtay, N., Lusk, L., Hayashi, K. M., Greenstein, D. Vaituzis, A. C., et al. (2004). Dynamic mapping of human cortical development during childhood through early adulthood. *Proceedings of the National Academy of Sciences, 101*(21), 8174–8179.

Goleman, D. (1995). *Emotional intelligence.* New York: Bantam Books.

Greenough, W. T., & Anderson, B. J. (1991). Cerebellar synaptic plasticity. Relation to learning versus neural activity. *Annals of the New York Academy of Sciences, 627,* 231–247.

Greenough, W. T., Withers, G., & Anderson, B. (1992). Experience-dependent synaptogenesis as a plausible memory mechanism. In I. Gormezano & E. A. Wasserman (Eds.), *Learning and memory: The behavioral and biological substrates* (pp. 209–229). Hillsdale, NJ: Erlbaum.

Hallowell, E. M., & Thompson, M. G. (1993). *Finding the heart of the child.* Washington, DC: National Association of Independent Schools.

Healy, J. (1990). *Endangered minds: Why our children don't think.* New York: Touchstone.

Hewson, M. G., & Hewson, P. W. (1983). Effect of instruction using students' prior knowledge and conceptual change strategies on science learning. *Journal of Research in Science Teaching, 20,* 721–743.

Introini-Collision, I. B., Miyazaki, B., & McGaugh, J. L. (1991). Involvement of the amygdala in the memory-enhancing effects of clenbuterol. *Psychopharmacology, 104*(4), 541–544.

Jancke, L. (2000). Cortical activations in primary and secondary motor areas for complex bimanual movements in professional pianists. *Cognitive Brain Research, 10*(1–2), 177–183.

Jenkins, J. R., Stein, M. L., & Wysocki, K. (1984). Learning vocabulary through reading. *American Educational Research Journal, 21*(4), 767–787.

Jernigan, T. L., & Tallal, P. (1990). Late childhood changes in brain morphology observable with MRI. *Developmental Medicine and Child Neurology, 32*(5), 379–385.

Johnson, D., & Johnson, R. (1984). *Learning together and learning alone: Cooperation, competition and individualization.* Englewood Cliffs, NJ: Prentice-Hall.

Johnson, D., & Johnson, R. (1992). Encouraging thinking through constructive controversy. In N. Davidson, & T. Worsham, (Eds.), *Enhancing thinking through cooperative learning.* New York: Teachers College Press, 120–137.

Kang, H., Shelton, D., Welcher, A., & Schuman, E. M. (1997). Neurotrophins and time: Different roles for TrkB signaling in hippocampal long-term potentiation. *Neuron, 19,* 653–664.

Kato, N., & McEwen, B. (2003). Neuromechanisms of emotions and memory. *Neuroendocrinology, 11,* 03, 54–58.

Koechlin et al. (1999). Relational memory by cross-curriculum. *Nature 399*(6732), 148–151.

Kohn, A. (1993). Why incentive plans cannot work. *Harvard Business Review, 71*(5), 54–63.

Kohn, A. (2004). Feel-bad education: The cult of rigor and the loss of joy. *Education Week, 24*(3), 36, 44.

Koutstaal, W., Buckner, R. L., Schacter, D., & Rosen, B. R. Fourth annual meeting of the Cognitive Neuroscience Society, March 23–25, 1997, Boston.

Kumar, D. D. (1991). A meta-analysis of the relationship between science instruction and student engagement. *Educational Review, 43*(1), 40–66.

Lavoie, R. (2005). *It's so much work to be your friend.* New York: Simon & Schuster.

Martin, R. C. (1993). Short-term memory and sentence processing: Evidence from neuropsychology. *Memory and Cognition, 21*(2), 173–183.

Martin, S. J., & Morris, R. G. M. (2002). New life in an old idea: The synaptic plasticity and memory hypothesis revisited. *Hippocampus 12,* 609–636.

McEwen, M (1999). Stress and hippocampal plasticity. *Annual Review of Neuroscience, 22,* 105–122.

McGaugh J. L., Introini-Collision, I. B., Nagahara, A. H., Cahill, L., Brioni, J. D., & Castellano, C. (1990). Involvement of the amygdaloid complex in neuromodulatory influences on memory storage. *Neuroscience and Biobehavioral Reviews, 14*(4), 425–431.

McGroarty, M. (1989). The benefits of cooperative learning arrangements in second language instruction. *National Association for Bilingual Association Journal, 13*(2), 127–143.

Meece, J. L., Wigfield, A., & Eccles, J. S. (1990). Predictors of math anxiety and its influence on young adolescents' course enrollment intentions and performance in mathematics. *Journal of Educational Psychology, 8,* 60–70.

Mueller, C. M., & Dweck, C. S. (1998). Intelligence praise can undermine motivation and performance. *Journal of Personality and Social Psychology, 75*(1), 33–52.

Naime, J. S. (2002). Remembering over the short-term: The case against the standard model. *Annual Review of Psychology, 53*(2), 53–81.

Neisser, U., & Harsch, N. (1992). Phantom flashbulbs: False recollections of hearing news about Challenger. In E. Winograd & U. Neisse (Eds.), *Affect and accuracy in recall: Studies of "flashbulb" memories* (pp. 9–31). New York: Cambridge University Press.

Nunley, K. F. (2000). In defense of the oral defense. *Classroom Leadership, 3*(5), 60.

Nunley, K. F. (2002). Active research leads to active classrooms. *Principal Leadership, 2*(7), *53–61.*

Nuthall, G. (1999). The way students learn: Acquiring knowledge from an integrated science and social studies unit. *Elementary School Journal, 99*(4), 303–341.

Nuthall, G., & Alton–Lee, A. (1995). Assessing classroom learning. How students use their knowledge and experience to answer classroom achievement test questions in science and social studies. *American Educational Research Journal, 32*(1), 185–223.

O'Grady, W., Dobrovolsky, M., and Aronoff, M. (Eds.) (1997). *Contemporary linguistics: An introduction.* New York: St. Martin's Press.

Olds, J. (1992). Mapping the mind onto the brain. In F. Worden, J. Swazey, & G. Adelman, *The Neurosciences, Paths of Discovery.* Boston, MA: Birkhauser.

Olff, P. (1999). Stress, depression and immunity: The role of defense and coping styles. *Psychiatry Research, 85,*(1), 7–15.

Olsen, K. (1995). *Science continuum of concepts for grades K–6.* Kent, WA: Center for the Future of Public of Education.

O'Reilly, R., & Rudy, J. (2000). *Hippocampus, 10*(4), 389–397.

Parker, R. (2002). A place to belong. *Independent Schools Magazine, 50*(2).

Patrick, B. C., Skinner, E. A., & Connell, J. P. (1993). What motivates children's behavior and emotion? Joint effects of perceived control and autonomy in the academic domain. *Journal of Personality and Social Psychology, 65,* 781–791.

Pawlak, R., Magarinos, A. M., Melchor, J., McEwen, B., & Strickland, S. (2003, February). Tissue plasminogen activator in the amygdala is critical for stress–induced anxiety-like behavior. *Nature Neuroscience,* 168–174.

Peterson, P. L., Carpenter, T. P., & Fennema, E. (1989). Teachers' knowledge of students' knowledge in mathematics problem solving: Correlation and case analysis. *Journal of Educational Psychology, 91*(4), 558–569.

Pressley, M., Goodchild, F., Fleet, J., Zajchowski, R., & Evans, E. D. (1989). The challenges of classroom strategy instruction. *Elementary School Journal, 89,* 301–342.

Pressley, M., Symons, S., McDaniel, M., Snyder, B. L., & Turnure, J. E. (1998). Elaborative interrogation facilitates acquisition of confusing facts. *Journal of Educational Psychology, 80,* 268–278.

Pressley, M., Wood, E., Woloshyn, V., Martin, V., King, A., & Menke, D. (1992). Encouraging mindful use of prior knowledge: Attempting to construct explanatory answers facilitates learning. *Educational Psychologist, 27*(1), 91–109.

Pulvirenti, L. (1992). Neural plasticity and memory: Towards an integrated view. *Functional Neurology, 7*(6), 481–490.

Redfield, D. L., & Rousseau, E. W. (1981). A meta-analysis of experimental research on teacher questioning behavior. *Review of Educational Research, 51*(2), 237–245.

Reeve, J. (1996). The interest-enjoyment distinction in intrinsic motivation. *Motivation and Emotion, 13,* 83–103.

Reeve, J., & Bolt, E. (1999, September). Student-centered classrooms and the teaching styles they exhibit. *The Journal of Educational Psychology, 91*(3), 537–548.

Robinson, D. H., & Kiewra, K. A. (1996). Visual argument: Graphic organizers are superior to outlines in improving learning from text. *Journal of Educational Psychology, 87*(3), 455–467.

Rose, F. D., Davey, M. J., & Attree, E. A. (1993). How does environmental enrichment aid performance following cortical injury in the rat? *Neuroreport, 4*(2), 163–166.

Rosenthal, R., & Jacobson, L. (1992). *Pygmalion in the classroom: Teacher expectation and pupils' intellectual development.* New York: Irvington.

Ross, J. A. (1988). Controlling variables: A metaanalysis of training studies. *Review of Educational Research, 58*(4), 405–437.

Rossi, E. L., & Nimmons, D. (1991). *The 20-minute break: Reduce stress, maximize performance, and improve health and emotional well-being using the new science of ultradian rhythms.* Los Angeles: Tarcher.

Rubin, B. (2005, March 10). American kids gorging on a diet of media, report finds. *Chicago Tribune,* p. 1.

Ryan, A. (1998). Why do some students avoid asking for help? *Journal of Educational Psychology, 90*(3), 528–535.

Schab, F. R. (1990). Odors and the remembrance of things past. *Journal of Experimental Psychology: Learning, Memory and Cognition, 16*(4), 648–655.

Schmuck, R. A., & Schmuck, P. A. (1983). *Group processes in the classroom.* Dubuque, IA: William C. Brown.

Schneider, W. (1993). Varieties of working memory as seen in biology and in connectionist/control architectures. *Memory and Cognition, 21*(2), 184–192.

Seeman, P. (1999). Images in neuroscience. Brain development, X: Pruning during development. *American Journal of Psychiatry, 156,* 168.

Sirevaag, A. M., & Greenough, W. T. (1991). Plasticity of GFAP-immunoreactive astrocyte size and number in visual cortex of rats reared in complex environments. *Brain Research, 540*(1–2), 273–278.

Slavin, R. E., (1983). *Cooperative learning.* New York: Longman.

Sousa, D. (2000). *How the brain learns: A classroom teacher's guide.* Thousand Oaks, CA: Corwin Press

Sowell, E. R., Peterson, B. S., & Thompson, P. M. (2003). Mapping cortical change across the human life span. *Nature Neuroscience 6,* 309–315.

Squire, L. R. (1992). Memory and the hippocampus: A synthesis from findings with rats, monkeys, and humans. *Psychological Review, 99*(2), 195–231.

Stickgold, R. (2000). *Nature Neuroscience, 3*(12), 1237–1238.

Vallerand, R. J., Fortier, M. S., & Guay, F. (1997). Self-determination and persistence in a real-life setting: Toward a motivational model of high school dropout. *Journal of Personality and Social Psychology, 72,* 1161–1176.

Van Overwalle, F., & De Metsenaere, M. (1990). The effects of attribution-based intervention and study strategy training on academic achievement in college freshmen. *British Journal of Educational Psychology, 60,* 299–311.

Wagner, A., Schacter, D., Rotte, M., Koutstaal, W., Maril, A., Dale, A. M., et al. (1998). Building memories: Remembering and forgetting of verbal experiences as predicted by brain activity. *Science, 281,* 1185–1190.

Wallace, C. S., Killman, V. L., Withers, G. S., & Greenough, W. T. (1992). Increases in dendritic length in occipital cortex after 4 days of differential housing in weanling rats. *Behavioral and Neural Biology, 58*(1), 64–68.

Webb, D., & Webb, T. (1990). *Accelerated learning with music.* Norcross, GA: Accelerated Learning Systems.

Webb, M. W., Nemer, M. N., & Chizhik, A. W. (1998). Equity issues in collaborative group assessment: Group composition and performance. *American Educational Research Journal, 17,* 607–651.

Werner, E., & Smith, R. (1989). *Vulnerable but invincible: A longitudinal study of resilient children and youth.* New York: Adams, Bannister, and Cox.

Wiersma, U. J. C. (1992). The effects of extrinsic reward on intrinsic motivation: A meta-analysis. *Journal of Occupational and Organizational Psychology, 65,* 101–110.

Willoughby, T., Desmarias, S., Wood, E., Sims, S., & Kalra, M. (1997). Mechanisms that facilitate the effectiveness of elaboration strategies. *Journal of Educational Psychology, 89*(4), 682–685.

Wolfson, A. (1998). Sleep schedules and daytime functioning in adolescents. *Child Development, 69*(4), 875–887.

Woloshyn, V. E., Willoughby, T., Wood, E., & Pressley, M. (1990). Elaborative interrogation facilitates adult learning of factual paragraphs. *Journal of Educational Psychology, 82,* 513–524.

Wunderlich, K., Bell, A., & Ford, A. (2005). Improving learning through understanding of brain science research. *Learning Abstracts, 8*(1). Available: www.league.org/publication/abstracts/learning/lelabs200501.html.

INDEX

Note: An *f* after a page number indicates a figure.

ABOUT THE AUTHOR

Dr. Judy Willis, a board certified neurologist and middle school teacher in Santa Barbara, California, has combined her training in neuroscience and neuroimaging with her teacher education training and years of classroom experience. She has become an authority in the field of learning-centered brain research and classroom strategies derived from this research.

After graduating Phi Beta Kappa as the first woman graduate of Williams College, Willis attended UCLA School of Medicine, where she remained as a resident and was ultimately Chief Resident in Neurology. She was in private practice for 15 years, and then received a credential and master's degree in education from the University of California, Santa Barbara. She has taught in elementary, middle, and graduate schools; was a fellow in the National Writing Project; and currently teaches at Santa Barbara Middle School. Her articles about the neurology of learning have been published in many educational journals. She has spoken at professional educator conferences and is completing a second book for educators about research-based strategies for special needs students in inclusive classrooms.

Willis is also a regular contributor to wine literature and writes wine columns for two newspapers. Her 2005 article in *Decanter* magazine described the impact of the film *Sideways* on California Pinot Noir sales. She can be reached by e-mail at jwillisneuro@aol.com.

Related ASCD Resources: The Brain and Learning

At the time of publication, the following ASCD resources were available; for the most up-to-date information about ASCD resources, go to www.ascd.org. ASCD stock numbers are noted in parentheses.

Multimedia
The Human Brain Professional Inquiry Kit by Bonnie Benesh (#999003)

Networks
Visit the ASCD Web site (www.ascd.org) and search for "networks" for information about professional educators who have formed groups around various topics, including "Brain-Compatible Learning." Look in the "Network Directory" for current facilitators' addresses and phone numbers.

Online Courses
Go to ASCD's Home Page (www.ascd.org) and click on professional development to find the following ASCD Professional Development Online Courses: The Brain: Memory and Learning Strategies, The Brain: Understanding the Mind, and The Brain: Understanding the Physical Brain.

Print Products
Educational Leadership November 1998 How the Brain Learns (#198261)
Brain-Based Learning Electronic Topic Pack (#197194)
Brain Matters: Translating Research into Classroom Practice by Patricia Wolfe (#101004)
Education on the Edge of Possibility by Geoffrey Caine and Renate Nummela Caine (#19702)
How to Teach So Students Remember by Marilee Sprenger (#105016)
Learning & Memory: The Brain in Action by Marilee Sprenger (#199213)
Teaching to the Brain's Natural Learning Systems by Barbara K. Givens (#101075)
Teaching with the Brain in Mind, 2nd edition by Eric Jensen (#198019)

Videotapes
The Brain and Learning (4 videos) (#498062)
The Brain and Mathematics (2 videos) (#400237)
The Brain and Reading (3 videos) (#499207)

For more information, visit us on the World Wide Web (www.ascd.org), send an e-mail message to member@ascd.org, call the ASCD Service Center (1-800-933-ASCD or 703-578-9600, then press 2), send a fax to 703-575-5400, or write to Information Services, ASCD, 1703 N. Beauregard St., Alexandria, VA 22311-1714 USA.